Teaching for Flow

Flow in positive psychology describes a mental state of being fully immersed and energised in the successful performance of a task. *Teaching for Flow* explores a radical transformation of the primary curriculum with a look at adopting a thematic, investigatory approach based on the children's interests, exploring ways to foster the right conditions for children to enter into the optimal state for learning, known as "flow" or more colloquially as "being in the zone".

Practical activities and classroom resources encourage deeper engagement and motivation among all students, regardless of their backgrounds or neurodiversity whilst simultaneously cultivating a love for learning, critical thinking and creativity. Informed by neuroscience, areas covered include learning and development, teaching for flow, special educational needs (SEND), outdoor learning and Forest School, homework and integrating flow into the curriculum. This book suggests a complete overhaul of the current curriculum to place emphasis on a more child-centred and engaging learning experience. Focusing on curriculum design and lesson planning and assessment, the author demonstrates how this inclusive approach can be applied practically, and how teachers can have autonomy over curriculum content driven by the interests of their pupils.

Teaching for Flow is an essential resource for any classroom teacher or school leader looking to develop a more active, investigatory and child-centred approach to learning in their school that allows children to grow and flourish.

Rebecca Meager is an experienced Primary School Teacher and Forest School Leader. After nearly 20 years working in UK primary schools, she left the classroom to follow her passion for the great outdoors and founded her own small Forest School business, Squirrel Scamps Forest School in Oxfordshire, UK.

Teaching for Flow

Transforming Primary Education for Optimal Learning

Rebecca Meager

LONDON AND NEW YORK

Designed cover image: Getty images

First published 2026
by Routledge
4 Park Square, Milton Park, Abingdon, Oxon OX14 4RN

and by Routledge
605 Third Avenue, New York, NY 10158

Routledge is an imprint of the Taylor & Francis Group, an informa business

© 2026 Rebecca Meager

The right of Rebecca Meager to be identified as author of this work has been asserted in accordance with sections 77 and 78 of the Copyright, Designs and Patents Act 1988.

All rights reserved. No part of this book may be reprinted or reproduced or utilised in any form or by any electronic, mechanical, or other means, now known or hereafter invented, including photocopying and recording, or in any information storage or retrieval system, without permission in writing from the publishers.

For Product Safety Concerns and Information please contact our EU representative GPSR@taylorandfrancis.com. Taylor & Francis Verlag GmbH, Kaufingerstraße 24, 80331 München, Germany.

Trademark notice: Product or corporate names may be trademarks or registered trademarks, and are used only for identification and explanation without intent to infringe.

British Library Cataloguing-in-Publication Data
A catalogue record for this book is available from the British Library

ISBN: 978-1-041-01895-7 (hbk)
ISBN: 978-1-041-01894-0 (pbk)
ISBN: 978-1-003-61684-9 (ebk)

DOI: 10.4324/9781003616849

Typeset in Optima
by codeMantra

Contents

Acknowledgements	vi
1 A Desire for Change	1
2 Understanding the Brain, Learning and Development	12
3 The Concept of "Flow"	20
4 Special Educational Needs and Disabilities: Why Our Most Vulnerable Children Could Benefit from a Curriculum That Engineers "Flow"?	26
5 Challenging the Doubts	36
6 Rethinking Homework for Engagement and "Flow"	55
7 The Benefits of Outdoor Learning	62
8 The Curriculum	83
9 Continuous Provision	114
10 Planning for "Flow"	123
11 Meaningful Assessment: Focusing on the Whole Child	138
12 Conclusion	150
Index	155

Acknowledgements

A heartfelt thanks to the numerous children and their families, dedicated colleagues and teachers who helped to stoke the fire within me – this book is for you! To my husband Gareth, family and friends, for supporting and encouraging me throughout, without you there would be no book. To Joy Baker for being such a huge inspiration to me. I'd also like to acknowledge the use of generative AI (Chat GPT version 4), which was a useful tool in helping me to explore and generate ideas in the face of a radical change, in parts of this book.

A Desire for Change

Passion and a desire to no longer sit back and accept the way our education system is not adequately serving our modern-day pupils has forced my mind to be thinking, if I had the power to make significant and groundbreaking changes to primary education, what would it look like?

It has been reported on the news in recent times how many of our children with special educational needs and disabilities (SEND) are being failed by the current systems. A lack of special school places and mainstream schools having limited resources means they are often unable to provide suitable provision for our most in need children. The current cohorts who are of school age now are still battling against the effects that COVID-19 had on learning during that time, including children starting school with delayed speech and language skills. The workforce is broken, constantly being battered negatively in the media and many people are unaware of the reality of the increasing workload for teachers, nearly always using the number of holidays as a counterargument. Teachers are working long hours (often working around 12 hours a day, when work taken home is considered) and in many cases expected to give more for no more pay which has and is still having a detrimental impact on teacher well-being.

> Primary classroom teachers worked longer hours – 59.3 hours – than their secondary school counterparts, who worked for 55.7 hours per week. The hours in a secondary academy were slightly less, at 55.2 hours.
>
> (*BBC News*, 2014)

When we think about well-being in particular, OFSTED has been in the headlines surrounding their impact on the well-being of staff after the most tragic death of Ruth Perry, something that caught the attention of everyone and yet not enough has changed as an outcome. The problem being that OFSTED have no regulatory body themselves, only having themselves to answer to and so when problems arise, there is no other layer that exists to investigate, challenge or monitor them. It is important to remember that the coroner ruled that OFSTED were found to have contributed towards the death of Ruth Perry in this instance. It is somewhat scandalous to see that the then Head of OFSTED, Amanda Spielman, has since been awarded a peerage. Importantly, the well-being of our children is also in decline. All of this put together emphasises the need for drastic change with the current overall system.

A Brief History

If we take a moment to look back through history, how much has our education system already changed and what impact has that had? Let's start in 1870 when the very first piece of legislation came in, "The 1870 Education Act".

> In this fundamentally important Act (the 'Forster Act'), the government finally accepted responsibility for the education of the nation's children. It was, however, only the start of a process which would take more than twenty years to complete.
>
> (Gillard, 2013)

The intention behind this act was a good one. It was a way of ensuring provision was available to offer everyone an education. Before this, education was limited to a small percentage of privileged children. Nevertheless, the introduction of this act appeared to be the start of the school curriculum becoming more restrictive with a greater emphasis on reading, writing and maths and the introduction of testing which came with rote learning. Teachers of the time were not enamoured with this new system.

> Teachers objected partly to the method of testing, but mainly to the principle of payment by results because it linked money for schools

with the criterion of a minimum standard. Thus, the higher quality primary work which was beginning to appear in the best elementary schools before 1861 was seriously discouraged.

(CPBML, 2020)

It is evident that since this time new strategies have come and gone, advances in technology meant that many changes have taken place in terms of equipment and curriculum being taught and of course behaviour management strategies have seen the thankful demise of a corporal punishment system. One strategy, in particular, that really sticks with me was the introduction of the Literacy and Numeracy hour (Back in the early 2000s), where you could be reprimanded for running over the hour. What if the children were really getting something out of that lesson? What if they were in "flow"? We will look more closely at what "flow" is later but, for now, a simple explanation would be that it is a state of engagement that you find yourself in where learning becomes effortless and "sticks" with fewer repetitions.

> Flow is an optimal psychological state that people experience when engaged in an activity that is both appropriately challenging to one's skill level, often resulting in immersion and concentrated focus on a task. This can result in deep learning and high levels of personal and work satisfaction.
>
> (Krist2366, 2014)

Historically, the purpose of education was largely centred around preparing students for their expected roles in society. This often meant that boys and girls were guided towards different subjects based on traditional gender roles. Boys were encouraged to develop practical skills in subjects such as woodworking, metalwork and technical drawing and were areas that aligned with careers in trades and industry. Meanwhile, girls were steered towards subjects like home economics, sewing and childcare, reinforcing the expectation that their primary role would be in managing a household and raising children.

As societal attitudes evolved and gender equality gained prominence, the separation between the education of boys and girls significantly diminished. Today, there is a much stronger emphasis on providing equal learning opportunities for all, regardless of gender. While some differences still exist, such as the necessary separation of P.E. lessons in secondary schools for biological and practical reasons, boys and girls are now encouraged to participate in the same academic and extracurricular activities.

The shift away from rigid gender-based learning has opened up far greater opportunities for all students. No longer are girls restricted to domestic skills while boys engage in hands-on technical subjects. Instead, schools now promote a broader, more inclusive curriculum where students are free to explore a diverse range of skills and interests. For example:

STEM Education (Science, Technology, Engineering and Mathematics): In the past, these subjects were often dominated by boys, while girls were not encouraged or expected to pursue careers in science and engineering. Today, there is a significant push to encourage both girls and boys to explore STEM fields, be this through school trips, companies who bring lessons into schools or through after school clubs. Beyond the classroom, the growing popularity of games such as Roblox and Minecraft as well as elaborate science kits available to buy provide children with STEM experiences outside of school too. Looking back to a few years ago, television shows like "Robot Wars" also played a role in inspiring young minds, both for boys and girls.

Home Economics: Once considered a "girls' subject", home economics is a subject that all pupils are now involved in. With an increased knowledge of nutrition and the integration of cuisines from around the world as well as designer clothes brands being popular among youngsters, the subject has evolved to be broader and perhaps of greater interest to both girls and boys alike. There are also influential figures involved of all genders which lends a role model for children to aspire to such as top chefs or clothes designers.

Creative and Practical Arts: Boys who might have once been steered away from activities like dance and who may well have been directed instead to sports such as football are now encouraged to explore creative fields without stigma. In the same way, girls are welcomed into traditionally male-dominated disciplines like woodwork, mechanics and engineering and design technology.

By breaking free from outdated gender expectations, education becomes more open to a culture where students could be encouraged to pursue their interests based on their own passion and aptitude rather than societal norms. This shift is crucial, not only in allowing students to develop a broader range of skills but also in challenging stereotypes. When young people see that they are not limited by gender in their educational choices, they are more likely to carry that confidence into their career decisions, leading to a more diverse and equitable workforce.

While progress has been made, there is still work to be done to ensure true equality in education. Subtle biases and societal expectations continue to influence subject choices, particularly at the secondary and higher education levels. However, by continuing to challenge these norms and encouraging all students to explore their full potential, we move closer to an education system that truly empowers every learner, regardless of gender.

The Tripartite System, introduced in the 1940s, divided secondary school children into three groups, placing them into different types of schools based on their abilities as determined by the 11+ exam. This meant children were effectively pigeonholed in terms of their potential while still in their final year of primary school.

Although the 11+ exam (also known as the Secondary Transfer Test) no longer applies nationwide, it still exists in selective areas like Buckinghamshire, where children must achieve a score of at least 121 to secure a grammar school place. The Buckinghamshire Government website notes that children who fall short of this score may still be considered if they receive Free School Meals (FSM) or Pupil Premium Funding, but these places are extremely limited.

It seems absurd to categorise children so rigidly at such a young age, especially when we acknowledge that children develop and flourish in their own time. The system sends a damaging message – that children are either "successful" or they are not. This can either discourage them from trying altogether or, conversely, foster resilience and determination to break free from the metaphorical straight jacket imposed on them by a single test on a single day.

Comparing grammar schools with comprehensive or secondary modern schools is inherently unfair. While grammar schools consistently outperform their non-selective counterparts in exam results, this advantage could be largely due to their selective intake rather than superior teaching or resources. A truly fair comparison would assess progress made from students' starting points, rather than raw results. Otherwise, it's like declaring victory in a race when you've started halfway down the track.

Many famously successful individuals failed or did poorly – only achieving a small number of pass grades – in their school exams yet went on to achieve remarkable things. Sir Richard Branson (British Entrepreneur) Sir Alan Sugar (English Business Entrepreneur), and Simon Cowell (English Record Executive and TV Personality) are just a few examples. It raises an important question: how many talented individuals may have been discouraged from reaching their full potential simply because they were placed in a restrictive category too early in life?

The 1980s saw the introduction of the National Curriculum, a significant shift in education policy. The then Prime Minister, Margaret Thatcher, who, incidentally, won a scholarship to Grammar school, made education reform a priority. In doing so, she stripped schools of much of their autonomy in designing their own curriculum, increasing central government control over what was taught. Thatcher and her government were critical of what they saw as a decline in educational standards due to progressive teaching methods that, in their view, allowed too much flexibility.

As a result, politicians with no background in education, beyond their own school experiences, made sweeping judgements that disregarded the expertise of those working on the ground: the teachers. Many educators strongly opposed these changes, particularly the introduction of SATs, which accompanied the National Curriculum. And who could blame them? The freedom they once had to engage students with content that sparked their curiosity and maximised their potential was abruptly taken away, like a rug pulled from beneath their feet.

I can't help but wonder: what if we had been on the right path before this intervention? Who's to say that experienced teachers, through their collective knowledge and first-hand understanding of their pupils, wouldn't have continued to refine and innovate education without the need for government interference? The message seemed clear, teachers' professional judgements and experience did not count. The government would take control (echoes of Boris Johnson's Brexit rhetoric "take back control"), even if that control was based on a limited and arguably ill-informed perspective.

That's not to say curiosity and a drive for improvement are inherently bad. But shouldn't experts in the field be consulted? Shouldn't all relevant facts be gathered before implementing such a major reform? Surely, a well-informed decision, based on professional insight rather than personal schooling experiences, would have been the more responsible course of action.

Teaching during this era (before the introduction of the national curriculum) was still largely characterised by a teacher-centred approach, where educators were the primary source of knowledge and pupils were passive learners. However, with the introduction of the National Curriculum, this approach became even more restrictive. Teachers, once skilled in crafting a meaningful and relevant curriculum, found themselves reduced to implementers of a rigid framework. Their professional judgement about what topics would be most valuable to their students was effectively sidelined.

The introduction of SATs and league tables further shifted the focus towards measurable outcomes at the expense of broader educational goals, such as social and emotional development, creativity and innovation, practical life skills, ethical and moral reasoning and critical thinking. While teachers gradually developed creative ways to reintegrate these elements, the emphasis remained heavily on tested subjects. Even today, despite recognising the importance of these broader skills, there is still not enough autonomy granted to teachers to allow their full potential to be realised. I would even venture to say that there is a danger that the more prescriptive we are about what it is we want teachers to teach we will in effect end up deskilling them in the process. Teaching is a practiced skill which matures with experience leading to deeper understanding and greater innovation. However, without the space and freedom for this development to happen, we risk creating a void in the effective evolution of education.

Education should be a dynamic, evolving process, shaped by those who understand its nuances best – the teachers. The question remains: how much further could we have come if their voices had been truly heard?

The Introduction of Academies and Free Schools

In the 2000s, academies were introduced in England as a means of improving schools deemed to be "inadequate" by Ofsted. Before this, such schools would be placed into special measures, triggering more frequent inspections, potential changes in staffing or of the governing body, and, in some cases, eventual closure. It is worth noting that Ofsted's role is merely to evaluate a school's effectiveness. To support improvement, it was down to local authorities to provide leadership mentoring, and most schools had a school improvement adviser who assessed performance, identified areas for improvement and recommended changes by working with the school to create development plans.

Academies differ in that they are independent of local authorities, run by academy trusts and state-funded but with greater autonomy over their operations. With the expansion of the academy system, multi-academy trusts

(MATs) have emerged, offering advantages such as shared resources and enhanced career progression for staff, particularly beneficial at a time when many schools face financial strain.

However, the core issue remains educational performance and student outcomes – the very reason we teach. Interestingly, when examining the data, there is no conclusive evidence that academies outperform local authority-maintained schools. In fact, a 2022 study found:

> 92% of council-maintained schools were rated 'Outstanding' or 'Good' by Ofsted as of 31 January 2022, compared to 85% of academies that were graded after conversion.
>
> (Eichler, 2022)

In a policy shift led by then Education Secretary Gillian Keegan, the government recently dropped plans to compel all schools to convert to academies by 2030, citing a need to focus on economic stability. The Academies Act 2010, introduced by Michael Gove, originally aimed to expand academy status beyond just failing schools, giving them greater autonomy.

However, the extent of this autonomy remains debatable. While academies have control over budgets, staff pay and curriculum design, they are still bound by Department for Education (DfE) policies, targets and initiatives. Though they are not required to follow the National Curriculum, they must provide a "broad and balanced" curriculum, covering core subjects like English, Maths and Science. This flexibility is, perhaps, a step forward, but the continued emphasis on standardised testing and government oversight limits the true extent of their independence which could in effect be hindering them and affecting the overall outcomes.

Similar to academies, free schools are government-funded but operate independently of local authorities. The key distinction is that while academies are existing schools that convert to independent status, free schools are entirely new institutions, often established by parents, teachers, charities, universities, businesses or community and faith organisations. Like academies, they are not required to follow the national curriculum.

Free schools were introduced in 2010 under the Academies Act, with the goal of offering parents more choice and increasing competition between schools – theoretically driving up standards and providing a higher quality of education. However, research suggests that the reality has not always lived up to this vision.

A study conducted by UCL's Faculty of Education and Society challenges the effectiveness of free schools in delivering superior education. Their findings state:

> On the aim of opening 'high quality' schools, we have shown free schools during our analysis period were not on average of high quality. This was particularly true of primaries.
>
> (Higham et al., 2024, p. 97)

This raises important questions about the effectiveness of free schools in improving educational outcomes. While greater choice and flexibility were at the heart of the initiative, inconsistent quality and variable student progress suggest that structural changes alone do not guarantee success. Instead of focusing solely on competition, perhaps the emphasis should shift towards evidence-based strategies for school improvement, ensuring that all students, regardless of the type of school they attend, receive a high-quality education.

Steering the System: The Role of an Education Secretary

The overseeing of the entire education system right from Early Years through to Higher Education is a hefty role. It is a role that entails the setting of national policy, the allocation of funding, the decision of curriculum content and the architect of educational reform. All of this responsibility rests upon the shoulders of the Education Secretary, making it one of the most influential positions in shaping the educational landscape of the country.

Since the start of my teaching career in 2004, I have seen 14 different Education Secretaries come and go – seven of them in just the past five years. To say this role has experienced high turnover is an understatement. How can we expect consistency, stability or long-term progress when those in charge barely have time to grasp the scale of the job before being replaced?

Some held the position for such brief periods that they barely made a dent. One such example was Michelle Donelan, who was Education Secretary for just two days in July 2022. Who? Exactly. Blink, and you missed her.

For an Education Secretary to make meaningful, positive change, it would make sense for them to exhibit the following qualities:

- Previous relevant experience from which they have gained a deep understanding of the Education system.
- An in-depth knowledge of current research in the field along with a vision of how this could be implemented.
- To be forward thinking by putting in place long-term strategies simply because any changes need time to embed and show any impact.

Yet, most Education Secretaries arrive with little to no hands-on experience in education, aside from attending school themselves as children. This raises the question: how can we expect impactful, informed decisions when those in charge lack first-hand experience?

If anything, this makes it even more crucial that the voices of experienced teachers, school leaders and education professionals are not just heard but actively involved in shaping policy. After all, they are the real experts. Until we recognise that, the cycle of instability is likely to continue, possibly at the expense of students, teachers and the very future of education itself.

It seems to me that we need to focus more on what research has taught us about how we, as humans, learn best and completely reform the curriculum to make it more child led, more engaging, less teaching to the tests and ultimately a far more effective, well-rounded education system where everyone feels they can achieve. Dive into the following pages to find out more about what the research tells us and explore how we could change our whole approach for the better.

References

BBC News. (2014, April 19). What hours do teachers really work? [online]. *BBC*. Available at: https://www.bbc.co.uk/news/education-27087942#:~:text=A%20primary%20school%20teacher%20will%20spend%20on [Accessed 18 May 2024].

CPBML. (2020, April 4). *The 1870 Education Act: The road to universal education*. [online] Communist Party of Britain Marxist-Leninist. Available at: https://www.cpbml.org.uk/news/1870-education-act-road-universal-education#:~:text=Teachers%20objected%20partly%20to%20the%20method%20of%20testing%2C [Accessed 18 May 2024].

Eichler, W. (2022, May 10). Council-maintained schools perform better than academies, report finds. [online] *LocalGov*. Available at: https://www.localgov.co.uk/Council-maintained-schools-perform-better-than-academies-report-finds/54161 [Accessed 14 Feb. 2025].

Gillard, D. (2013, February 18) *Elementary Education Act 1870 – Full text.* [online] Education in the UK. Available at: https://www.education-uk.org/documents/acts/1870-elementary-education-act.html [Accessed 4 June 2025].

Higham, R., Anders, J., Chouhy, G., Green, F., Henseke, G. and McGinity, R. (2024). *The Free Schools Experiment: Analysing the Impacts of English Free Schools.* UCL Faculty of Education and Society. Available at: https://discovery.ucl.ac.uk/id/eprint/10195862/ [Accessed 6 June 2025].

Krist2366. (2014, August 22) *Flow (Csíkszentmihályi) in learning theories.* [online] Learning-Theories.com. Available at: https://learning-theories.com/flow-csikszentmihalyi.html [Accessed 6 June 2025].

Understanding the Brain, Learning and Development

When we think about intellectual development, we think of a person's ability to receive, retain and use an ever-growing amount of information. After all, this is what our school system would have us believe when so often it is steered solely towards passing the next set of tests. However, intellectual development is not merely about information and knowledge retention, it is also about progressing through trial, error and problem-solving, developing a self-assurance to be able to utilise this safely, growing towards an increasing independence. Creativity is also extremely important, which I would define as using what we already know to create something that is original and meaningful. This doesn't even have to be a physical object; it might be a spoken sentence or a description of a made-up creature. In fact, allowing time for creativity and learning through play for children up to 11 years old is an essential part of cognitive development.

> Creative and artistic play helps with learning and development by letting children engage in problem solving where there are no right answers. With creative activity, the process is more important than the end product.
>
> (Fraserhealth, 2018)

The Importance of Play

Play engages children in learning in a way that is both contextual and meaningful. It is unforced, often so joyful and absorbing that it doesn't feel like learning at all. When a young child is learning through play, they are fully immersed – their brains active, their synapses firing. In these moments, children naturally practice and refine the skills they need to take their play further. For example, they might practise writing by making signs for a den that reads "Keep Out!" or explore cause and effect by repeatedly jumping in a puddle and noticing the splash it creates.

Through play, children also learn to differentiate for themselves. They solve problems, adapt games and modify challenges to match their ability and confidence. A child might tweak the rules of a chasing game to add a "safe base" or push themselves to perfect a cartwheel at breaktime, asking friends for feedback. These moments show children taking ownership of their learning including adjusting difficulty, seeking mastery and collaborating with peers.

In contrast, consider a child asked to sit on the carpet for a teacher-led learning task. Some children may appear engaged, yet their minds may wander, if the activity doesn't capture their interest. Others may show clear signs of disengagement such as fidgeting, calling out or struggling to remain seated. Even those who are focused can only sustain attention for a limited time in such a passive setting, particularly in the early years. With play, however, the duration of engagement is guided by each child's natural capacity for focus. They move on when their interest fades, rather than when an external instruction tells them to, allowing learning to happen on their own terms, at their own pace.

But how much meaningful play are our children able to engage in during the school day, particularly once they reach key stage 2? In my experience, very little. If we look more closely at the aspect of creativity and think about how this can be achieved and developed, it becomes apparent that there are many ways this can be done, but essentially scrapping a strict linear approach is key.

> Most education focuses on providing answers in a linear step by step way. Mobley realized that asking radically different questions in a non-linear way is the key to creativity.
> (Naiman, 2012 Updated 2024)

It strikes me that we are often over-prescriptive in our teaching methods. How often is it that a class of children, during an art lesson, for example, will all produce a similar version of the same picture? Let's take Vincent Van Gogh's Sunflower picture for example. The teacher creates a model, demonstrating techniques for recreating a version of the painting that the children must recreate for themselves in the same way. What learning may they have gained from that experience? They may have gained some knowledge of the artist Vincent Van Gogh, they would be able to recognise a famous painting and name the artist, they will have practised an art skill, maybe learned about mixing colours and/or learned about textures, depending on the focus of the lesson. There is no doubt that the children will have gained some knowledge and learning from this experience and some may have really enjoyed it, some may have merely reluctantly done the task to please the teacher. Have any of them developed they're creativity, problem-solving skills or imagination during that particular task? Was there really an opportunity given for this? Supposing we allowed for them to explore this image with more freedom. We could still do some teaching input about the artist and teaching about colour and/or texture but what if we then put out a wide selection of craft materials and asked them to recreate the picture in the way they choose. Your teaching inputs would then be "in the moment", going along with the children's ideas and teaching smaller groups specific techniques and skills based on their interests and preferences. For example, there may be a group of children who would like to paint the picture. A discussion could happen about what paint, what brush or other equipment? Are you going to add texture? What could you use to create the texture? You could even demonstrate examples to that group. Another group may decide to create a collage, another a sculpture etc. The end of the lesson could then focus on a discussion about the children's experiences – what did you do to create your picture? Which do we think is most effective? Why? And so on.

When we compare this approach, there is so much more learning that would come from a lesson such as this and as a bonus, less preparation and planning for the teacher as much of this is done in the moment. There would be problem-solving involved, exploration of a range of techniques, evaluation of methods and all of this happening naturally. In this scenario, because the children are owning the task, they are all more likely to become fully engaged and enter a state of "flow". It also creates a safer and more comfortable learning environment for children to make mistakes and learn from them because they are not working towards a "this is one I made earlier" example, where a feeling of failure can easily occur if the child's final piece does not look exactly like the modelled example.

When it comes to developing connections in the brain, this can be developed through problem-solving opportunities. A less prescriptive and more

Understanding the Brain, Learning and Development

child-led approach, lends itself to developing problem-solving skills in a way that is purposeful. If we go back to the Vincent Van Gogh, "sunflowers" example, possible problem-solving activities might consist of colour mixing to find the right colour, experimenting with different tools and techniques to get the right texture, trial and error with different materials etc.

Teamwork may be required as pupils learn from one another and help each other to create similar effects. Teamwork and co-operation are important for intellectual development because it involves a focus on co-creating ideas and developing solutions.

This approach could help our brains to be more receptive to taking on new information. It is the difference between being "told" a way forward and being allowed to "find" a way forward. When we "find" a way forward we are more likely to remember it and have a deeper overall understanding of the underlying "hows" and "whys" because of the process our brains go through to get there.

Exploring the Triune Brain Model: Foundations for Learning and Behaviour

To explain this, we first need to look at and understand a bit about neuroscience. Here we have a depiction of the Triune Model as proposed by neuroscientist Paul Maclean.

As shown in Figure 2.1, our brains have three different layers. The outer layer, neo cortex being the part that makes us human. It is the part that drives our impulse control, empathy and problem-solving. The middle layer, limbic layer, is the part that controls our emotions and relationships. The centre part, the reptilian brain, is the brain stem right at the "heart" of the brain and this controls all of our basic functions that happen without us thinking about them, such as breathing and the "fight or flight" response. The reptilian brain is the core, if you like, which is essentially the same in all of us. The brain contains a full set of neurons when we are born and as we begin to learn and make connections, we develop pathways between these neurons which become stronger the more we repeat them. Neurons that we don't use eventually disappear.

When we experience trauma, this can affect our brain function in that we rely more on the reptilian part of our brain, the essential part that keeps us alive. This can mean that for children who have experienced trauma, their "fight" or "flight" response maybe more easily triggered and when this

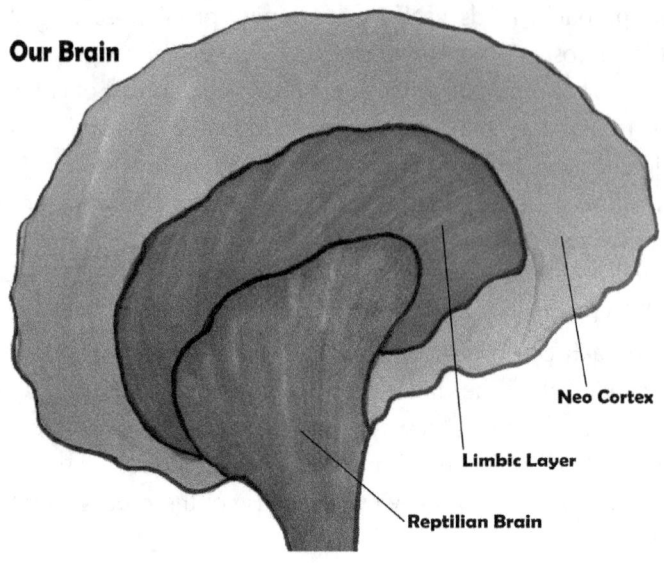

Figure 2.1 Illustrates the major layers of the brain, as proposed in the 1960s by Paul Maclean, which are linked to different functions as described in more detail below.

happens it makes it more difficult to take on new information as access to, and therefore development of, the other parts of the brain will be limited. These children will need to feel safe, comfortable and may need smaller, shorter tasks building up more slowly to more daunting tasks to enable them to learn and develop efficiently.

Research has shown that children who have missed out on experiences that help them to make these connections in the brain have gaps where neurons have died off due to not being used. This can cause problems for children who have these gaps when it comes to skills such as controlling emotions, forming relationships and problem-solving.

> Reciprocal serve and return interactions are essential—without them, the brain's architecture does not develop as expected, leading to long-term impacts on learning, behavior, and health.
> (Center on the Developing Child at Harvard University, 2025)

When we talk about a variety of experiences, we are talking about including all the senses in that process. The more senses involved, the more this helps the brain to form these connections.

As children grow, their way of thinking develops. Amanda Morin, in an online article entitled "How kids develop thinking and learning skills", writes about how children develop more logical thinking skills from the age of seven and become increasingly able to make connections, piecing clues together like a puzzle. She goes on to say:

> Socially, kids typically develop the ability to take turns, see other people's perspectives, and understand that actions have consequences. The circuits that process emotion and feelings strengthen and mature. At this stage, you can help kids along by teaching them to reflect on things like cause and effect.
>
> (Morin, 2019)

A simple activity such as solving a peg puzzle offers rich opportunities for brain development in a young child. As they begin to explore how different shapes fit into spaces, they develop visual and spatial awareness. At the same time, their fine motor skills are strengthened through the precise movements required to grip and manipulate the puzzle pieces. Hand-eye coordination is developed as they align each piece with its correct position, using both sight and touch. Through trial and error, they begin to problem-solve as they learn to rotate or adjust the pieces until they find a successful fit. As they repeat this process, memory is reinforced, and perseverance is nurtured, especially when their efforts are rewarded by the satisfying completion of the puzzle. What may seem like a simple task is, in fact, a powerful experience for forming and strengthening essential neural connections. Each of these processes activates different regions in the brain helping to form and strengthen the neural pathways that are essential for later learning.

There is growing concern about the increased use of technology and the amount of time children are spending on devices such as tablets and smartphones. With these tools now deeply embedded in everyday life, many children have regular access to screens from a very young age. While we do not yet fully understand the long-term effects of this shift on the developing brain, emerging research suggests it may be more harmful than we currently realise. Interestingly, brain scans have shown that when children are using technology, even when they appear highly engaged, only limited areas of the brain are activated. In contrast, hands-on activities like building a den stimulate far more widespread brain activity. This difference raises important questions about the quality of cognitive engagement provided by screen-based experiences. Overreliance on technology, particularly in early childhood, could potentially hinder the formation of strong neural connections, making it a cause for careful reflection and balance in children's daily lives.

Providing children with frequent opportunities to experiment, reflect on cause and effect and tackle problems as they arise naturally promotes deeper, more meaningful learning. When learners have the freedom to explore and differentiate their own learning experiences, rather than simply following a step-by-step model to recreate an idea, understanding is far more likely to "stick". This approach not only enhances engagement, but also nurtures resilience, independence and a genuine desire to take ownership of their learning journey.

Encouraging intellectual development in children requires more than just the traditional methods of knowledge retention and rote learning. It demands a holistic approach that includes creativity, problem-solving and experiential learning. By moving away from overly prescriptive teaching methods and allowing children to engage in meaningful, creative play and exploration, we can cultivate a learning environment that not only enhances healthy brain development but also encourages independence and resilience as they learn through trial-and-error methods. Embracing this approach aligns with our understanding of brain development, particularly the importance of creating and reinforcing neural connections through diverse and engaging experiences. Ultimately, when we prioritise creativity and child-led learning, we not only support academic success but also nurture well-rounded, inquisitive individuals ready to navigate the complexities of the world.

References

Center on the Developing Child at Harvard University. (2015). *Brain architecture.* [online] Center on the Developing Child, Harvard University. Available at: https://developingchild.harvard.edu/science/key-concepts/brain-architecture/#:~:text=The%20basic%20architecture%20of%20the%20brain%20is%20constructed [Accessed 5 June 2025].

Fraserhealth. (2018). *Intellectual development in children: How to encourage intellectual growth* [online] Fraserhealth.ca. Available at: https://www.fraserhealth.ca/health-topics-a-to-z/children-and-youth/intellectual-development-in-children [Accessed 5 June 2025].

Morin, A. (2019, August 6). *How kids develop thinking and learning skills.* [online] www.understood.org. Available at: https://www.understood.org/en/articles/how-kids-develop-thinking-and-learning-skills [Accessed 5 June 2025].

Naiman, L. (2012 updated 2024, February 16). *Can creativity be taught? Here's what the research says.* [online] Creativity at Work. Available at: https://www.creativityatwork.com/can-creativity-be-taught/ [Accessed 5 June 2025].

 The Concept of "Flow"

I was first introduced to the concept of "flow" by the book "Working with Emotional Intelligence" by Daniel Goleman which I read whilst training to be a Forest School leader. In his book (on page 106) he describes flow as "the ultimate motivator". He explains how following our interests pulls us into a flow state as we partake in the activities we enjoy doing. We are fully and effortlessly motivated to the point where the task at hand is a pleasure. He also points out that how and when we enter a state of "flow" will vary from person to person as we are unique individuals with our own passions, careers and skillsets.

Being in "flow" means you are in the optimal state for learning. Your brain is at a point of engagement that enables learning to take place with ease and requires far less repetition for that learning to embed. It was in fact Mihaly Csikszentmihalyi, a Hungarian-American psychologist who coined the term "flow". As I understand it, he visualised "flow" as an essential component leading to happiness, fulfilment and creativity. Ultimately, he found "flow" to be connected to high performance and improved well-being – the two outcomes that education continually strives to enhance for all pupils. And yet, his name is rarely spoken about in schools or teacher training. It was only through my own research sparked by my Forest School training, that I was introduced to this name and came across his ideas. Creating "flow" in the classroom requires more than just good planning – it demands the engagement of genuine interest from the learner, the right balance of challenge: not so easy that boredom sets in, but not so difficult that interest and enjoyment diminish leading to frustration. Achieving this delicate balance takes skill, precision and a deep understanding of the pupils as individuals.

The Concept of "Flow"

Many of us will experience "flow" in our occupations and hobbies. Think about those times when you have become so deeply absorbed in an activity that you lose track of time. It's possible that you had entered a state of "flow". Let's take a look at some examples:

A pianist at a concert: A pianist whether playing a well-known composition or a composition of their own would be completely absorbed in the music. For a pianist who may be composing their own piece of music they would be seamlessly creating and responding to the notes without conscious effort, signalling a state of "flow". The pianist may be so engaged that they lose track of time and may even forget the audience is there while they focus solely on the task at hand.

A footballer in a match: A footballer as he/she receives the ball and can make sight of a goal opportunity – his/her reactions become instinctive as he/she reacts to the opposing team's move and makes their shot with precision. They are absorbed in that moment and lost in a state of "flow".

A baker baking a birthday cake: When watching programmes on the television about cake baking and the amazing cakes that some people are capable of baking, you can see that the high-quality end product is derived from a deep focus and engagement in the task. From the effortless planning of the creation to the finished masterpiece, there will be many moments in the process where the baker will enter a "flow" state.

A teacher when planning lessons: There have definitely been times when during planning I have entered a state of "flow" – where ideas have arrived in a constant stream, the words have filled the page easily and I have felt an excitement about teaching it while writing. You notice when you are interrupted whilst in that "flow" state and must drag your focus back to other things for a while. At times like these, it can be difficult to fall back into that "flow" state again.

A police detective solving a crime: A police detective who is working on a challenging case, fully concentrated as they begin to connect the dots to solve the case and is guided by evidence and instinct. This high level of engagement leads to more efficient problem-solving which is crucial to a crime investigation where often time is of the essence.

These examples illustrate how being in a state of flow can enhance progress and performance across various fields, enabling individuals to achieve their best with ease and enjoyment.

"Flow" can occur in many everyday activities, not just in exceptional or high-stakes scenarios. Here are some examples of "flow" in everyday life:

Talking on the phone or having a conversation: Think of those times where you've been so caught up in conversation with a friend, perhaps it's a friend that you haven't seen for a while, that while you've been talking your tea has gone cold. You've been so wrapped up in the conversation that the time has passed by unnoticed.

A DIY project: Whether it's home improvements or building flat-packed furniture, there are times that you will get lost in the moment as you focus on the task at hand. The challenge in the task needs to be just right – not too much but also not too little – and that "flow" state will empower you in your task.

Getting lost in a book: For an avid reader, reading is a good example of entering a state of "flow". As you become lost in the pages of the book, and you are transported to a different place. You sink into the story feeling the emotion as you laugh or cry at what unfolds.

Exercise: Whether it's working out at the gym, taking part in a team sport or going for a run or walk, it is possible to experience a "flow" state. It might be the rhythmical movement, or perhaps the immersion of the game that sends you into that state where you are so absorbed that you may only realise how tired you are or how much your muscles ache when you have stopped.

Housework: For some, cleaning and organising can be a "flow" activity. The repetitive tasks of sorting, arranging and creating order can be extremely satisfying and immersive.

Doing a jigsaw puzzle: There will almost certainly be moments of "flow" whilst completing a jigsaw puzzle. Your attention and focus will be gripped by the need to find the "missing" piece and the satisfaction of finding each piece keeps you motivated holding you in this immersed state.

Engaging in a hobby: Many hobbies involve some form of creativity from playing a musical instrument to building a model train set in the loft. When you are deeply engaged in creating something you are likely to be in that state of "flow", where the world around you fades into the distance.

Playing a video game: Video games are often designed to offer the player an immersive experience. You become fully engrossed in the game you are playing as you overcome challenges and progress through levels.

The Concept of "Flow"

These examples show that "flow" can be a part of many activities that we encounter in our daily lives, often making everyday life more enjoyable and fulfilling. It is important to point out though that we may all experience "flow" during different activities. It is dependent on what you personally find the most engaging.

How does this relate to what we know about the brain and how can we use this knowledge to build a far more efficient education system? I refer again to Goleman in his book *Working with Emotional Intelligence* where he explains that the common scenario when people make difficult tasks look easy is often an outward sign that the brain has entered a state of "flow". He describes how "flow" "poses a neural paradox" where our brains can cope with more challenging tasks whilst in a state of "flow" compared with how our brains function in a more haphazard way when we are disinterested, distracted or in an anxious state. He goes on to state:

> But during flow, the brain appears efficient and precise in its pattern of firing. The result is an overall lowering of cortical arousal – even though the person may be engaged in an extremely challenging task.
> (Goleman, 1998, p. 107)

When we think back to what we know about how the brain needs to be in the optimal state for learning and we consider how this relates to "flow", this is something that needs to be thought about and utilised if we want to improve efficiency in our learning environments.

Nevertheless, when we reflect on the typical classroom environment and the structure of the school day, we must ask: how often do we genuinely create the conditions for "flow" to occur? Yes, there are some instances such as open-ended maths investigations as one example, where the children are able to experiment, explore strategies and engage in trial and error, providing motivation and purpose. However, if the majority of the time the children are passively following and carrying out over-prescriptive tasks that do not offer scope for creativity or problem-solving to flourish then the likelihood of entering a state of "flow" is significantly reduced. The over-emphasis on preparation for tests is one such example. If we consider that being in "flow" is the optimal state for learning, I think we can agree that there are often not enough opportunities presented to our pupils, particularly those in key stage 2, during the school day.

Having led Forest School sessions and regularly seen "flow" in action, I was really struck by what could be achieved in one afternoon with very little input. I've witnessed many creative moments such as where groups have spontaneously created their own songs and have gone on to using natural materials to create instruments to accompany them. Being given the freedom to experiment and better their performances each week, I could see the children setting their own challenges and progressing effortlessly. I've had groups of children discover how to build bridges, honing their problem-solving skills and learning what is needed to make them strong enough to hold their weight. They have learned the importance of working together, if they want the best den, they need the help and ideas of everyone.

This kind of learning, where mistakes are embraced as opportunities rather than feared, is, in my opinion, still rare in many classroom environments. Instead, a fear of "getting it wrong" often takes hold, which has long been recognised by educators as a major barrier to effective learning. In response, several initiatives have aimed to shift this mindset, most notably the introduction of *Growth Mindset* principles. This approach encourages children to understand that intelligence and ability are not fixed traits, and that with effort and persistence, improvement is always possible. The widely shared video *Austin's Butterfly* serves as a powerful example of how feedback, perseverance and a willingness to learn from mistakes can lead to meaningful growth.

There is no doubt that these ideas have value. But we must ask: how effective is it to simply talk to children about having a growth mindset? Are we truly embedding these principles in our classroom culture? For them to take root, the right conditions must be in place – ones that give children real agency, where they are motivated to grow because they *want* to, not just because they are told to. Otherwise, the growth mindset risks becoming just another passive instruction, rather than an authentic part of the learning process.

As teachers, we often begin a lesson with a clear and specific outcome in mind. While this helps ensure curriculum coverage and progression, it can unintentionally create an environment where there is little room for exploration, risk-taking or deviation from the intended path. This structure can foster a fear of failure, where children worry about giving the "wrong" answer or not meeting expectations. Under such conditions, the possibility for entering a state of "flow", where learning feels effortless, focused and intrinsically rewarding, is greatly reduced.

In contrast, "flow" appears to occur far more naturally and frequently in Forest School settings. This is largely due to the ethos and values at the heart of Forest School, where child-led learning is not only encouraged but celebrated. The Forest School leader observes children's play and interests closely, using these observations to guide the planning of activities or the introduction of new skills. Instead of imposing a rigid learning objective, they nurture each child's curiosity and personal fascinations, whether it's identifying a new plant, mastering a knot or constructing a sculpture inspired by Andy Goldsworthy.

Because children are given real autonomy in how they spend their time and what they focus on, their engagement deepens. When a child chooses to investigate something out of genuine interest or pursues a creative project with intrinsic motivation, they are far more likely to enter a state of "flow". In these moments, the learning becomes truly meaningful, absorbing, joyful and long-lasting. Forest School not only supports academic and developmental growth but also offers a valuable model for how we might rethink classroom learning to allow for more flexibility, autonomy and authentic engagement.

The concept of "flow" offers profound insights into optimising learning and performance, revealing how deeply engaging activities can elevate both enjoyment and efficiency. By understanding how "flow" states occur and their impact on the brain's functionality, we can reimagine educational environments to better foster these optimal conditions. Traditional classroom settings often lack opportunities for students to experience "flow", overshadowed by rigid structures and the fear of failure. However, experiences from some educational practices such as Forest School sessions highlight the immense potential of unstructured, exploratory learning, where creativity, collaboration and resilience are naturally cultivated. Embracing the principles of "flow" in educational systems can transform how students engage with learning, making it a delightful and deeply rewarding process. As educators, creating more opportunities for "flow" can lead to a more dynamic and effective approach to teaching, ultimately nurturing a generation of learners who are motivated, innovative and resilient.

Reference

Goleman, D. (1998) *Working with Emotional Intelligence*. Bloomsbury.

Special Educational Needs and Disabilities

Why Our Most Vulnerable Children Could Benefit from a Curriculum That Engineers "Flow"?

In the short time that I was SEND co-ordinator, I developed an insight into how our current system is not adequate and, in many cases, chronically broken when it comes to catering for many children with specific needs. It is not right that parents and schools must fight so hard to get even adequate schooling for their children and it became no surprise to me as to why many parents make the decision to home school their children.

The number of SEN pupils within our Primary Education system has been growing. According to NASEN the newest data as of July 2024 shows that a total of 18.4% of children up from 17.3% the previous year fall under this category. It is vitally important that we are providing a learning environment that is beneficial to all children within our system and that all are able to have a positive experience of school. With Emotionally Based School Avoidance on the rise, all too often, school becomes a morning battle for parents and their children particularly for children with additional needs. We need to question whether our current dated systems, learning environments and curriculum are still fit for purpose to accommodate this growing section of our modern society. It is plain to see that expecting them to fit the current mould is not working and is putting a strain not just on the children themselves, but also their families and the teachers as they deal with the behavioural implications and gaps in learning that come hand-in-hand with such situations.

In a previous chapter we have looked at the brain and how the right conditions and experiences are essential for cognitive development. But does this only apply to neurotypical learners? When we start to think about neurodiverse learners, including those who have experienced trauma, thinking about how the brain learns best is even more crucial. Neurodiverse learners may need to engage in specific individual behaviours such as making specific, repetitive movements known as "stimming" to help them to regulate before their brains are receptive to learning. We want them to be able to conduct these behaviours to help them and to ensure that they are not "masking" which can have a long-term impact on mental health. We all have "masking" behaviours to some extent to be able to fit in with society. I often used to say to my class, "When we are at school we have to behave in a certain way, I'm a different Mrs Meager to the Mrs Meager you would see at home". But for children who are neurodiverse it is a "need" to behave in certain ways in order for them to be able to function comfortably and without using extra effort and resources just to be able to focus on a task.

> The terms autism masking, to mask, act or camouflage are typically used to describe individuals who consciously and/or subconsciously hide their autistic behaviours and characteristics. Autistic people use masking as a means to manage the way people perceive them in social situations.
> (Kendall, 2020, p. 26)

The act of masking is completely exhausting and unfortunately our school system does not help. School rules, attitudes and the way in which schools function on a daily basis are deliberately designed to ensure all participants adhere to a set standard of behaviour – requiring them to "tow the line". Failure to comply results in imposed negative consequences. I deliberately use the word "imposed" because that is precisely what they are. These consequences might include being moved to another part of the classroom, being sent out of the room, a discussion with a senior staff member, missing break time, or involving parents. Importantly, these actions are something *done to* the child, rather than allowing the child to learn from the natural impact of their behaviour.

This is particularly evident with rules like wearing a school uniform. Such rules do not inherently carry a negative consequence. If a child chooses not to wear their uniform, the likelihood is that nothing naturally harmful or disruptive occurs. As a result, schools must create an artificial consequence to enforce compliance. This highlights a broader issue in many school systems – relying on externally imposed punishments to enforce rules rather than encouraging intrinsic understanding or learning from the natural outcomes of one's actions.

This means that, in order to follow school rules, children must develop a level of obedience that requires them to ignore their own reasoning and intrinsic motivation in favour of compliance with externally imposed expectations. Just as Naomi Fisher points out in her book *A Different Way to Learn*.

> To be successful in school, children have to learn a certain degree of passivity. They wait to be told what to do. They follow instructions.
> (Fisher, 2023, p. 104)

For neurodiverse children, this can be particularly challenging. Take the example of school uniforms: for a child with sensory hypersensitivities, wearing certain items, such as a collared shirt, can be intensely uncomfortable or even excruciating. Imagine trying to concentrate on a task while a pin is constantly pressing into your skin. No matter how engaging the task might be, your attention would be pulled away by the discomfort. Over time, you might learn to tolerate it or develop strategies to cope, but the discomfort wouldn't go away, and it could build to the point of overwhelming you emotionally. This is a helpful way to understand what touch sensitivity can feel like for some neurodiverse children. Everyday sensations like the texture of clothing, a tag on a shirt, or a light touch can be experienced as deeply uncomfortable or even painful. While these children may appear to be managing, the sensory distress remains in the background and can eventually lead to a meltdown or shutdown. Fortunately, many schools have adapted their policies to allow reasonable adjustments, such as permitting a plain white T-shirt instead of a collared shirt or polo shirt. This ensures that the uniform does not become a barrier to their learning or well-being. However, this is just one example of how current systems and expectations can unintentionally create obstacles for neurodiverse learners. It highlights the need for greater flexibility and understanding within educational environments to ensure all children can thrive.

There are many aspects of the overall school experience that can add significant extra challenge to daily life for children who are neurodiverse.

Special Educational Needs and Disabilities

I think Naomi Fisher paints the picture really well when she describes how the school system wrongly teaches you that "sitting still and keeping quiet" is what a successful learner does and that their personal interests are best kept for time outside of the classroom, be it in the playground at breaktime or at home. She says,

> They learn to ignore their own thought processes if they're "off-topic" – you can't start to investigate the history of domestic cats during a maths lesson, just because you saw one out of the window and it made you wonder if the ancient Egyptians kept cats. Schools call this keeping on task.
>
> (Fisher, 2023, p. 104)

These rules and expectations not only restrict the learning of many neurodiverse pupils, particularly when it comes to what are often labelled as "learning behaviours", but the rigid structure and time constraints of the school system also leave little room for pupils to pursue their natural interests as they arise. As teachers, we often encounter unexpected opportunities for learning, yet we frequently feel too constrained to embrace them. The pressure to ensure pupils meet specific lesson objectives or the need to stick to a strict timetable can stifle these moments of curiosity and exploration.

Consider, for example, a thunderstorm outside the classroom window. Suddenly, all attention is drawn to the storm. Some children may express fear, while others are eager to watch and learn. Their curiosity is sparked, and questions begin to flow: What causes a storm? What is lightning made of? Why does thunder make such a loud noise? For those experiencing fear, understanding the science behind storms could help alleviate their anxiety as fear often stems from the unknown.

Yet, in the current system, we often feel compelled to brush aside these moments, redirecting children back to the prescribed lesson plan. This approach seems counterproductive, as it overlooks the immense potential for meaningful and memorable learning that these spontaneous opportunities provide.

This reluctance to deviate from the established format, often due to external pressures put upon teachers, be it time constraints, curriculum demands or accountability measures, brings into question its impact on all learners, both neurodiverse and neurotypical. Children are, by nature, curious and constantly seek to make connections, even if those connections initially appear poorly timed or unrelated. Teachers will be all too familiar with the scenario during carpet time when a child raises their hand to share a story about a subject seemingly unrelated to the topic such as their pet cat. However, this interruption often reflects the child's attempt to link the lesson to their own experiences or its their way of trying to make connections. Children's brains are still developing and often dart around searching for such connections. For example, while counting objects in class, a child might suddenly recall that it's their cat's birthday and that their cat is the same age as the number they just counted to. This connection then leads their mind to wander, and they begin talking about their cat instead.

Children's questions and observations stem from a natural desire to make sense of the world around them. In their early years, they are naturally active learners, driven by curiosity, exploration and a need to understand. Yet within the rigid structure of many schools, creativity, innovation and independent thought are often stifled in favour of compliance and quiet obedience. Anything outside the expected norms may be perceived as chaotic or undisciplined, challenging the traditional view of what education is "supposed" to look like. This mindset risks suppressing the very qualities that enable children to think critically, solve problems and develop a lifelong love of learning. It is these qualities, the ones that make us beautifully unique, that should be nurtured, not subdued, within the classroom.

Another fundamental challenge within our current education system is its expectation that all pupils develop at the same rate, reaching identical milestones at the same time and age. When children don't meet these benchmarks, they are labelled as "behind", and interventions are often introduced. These interventions typically remove children from other learning activities to focus on what they have yet to grasp, based on the assumption that they should have mastered it by now.

Let's consider why this approach can be counterproductive. Take potty training as an example. Parents who have been through this stage with their young children quickly discover that the age at which a child is fully potty-trained, that is, dry during both day and night, varies greatly. It is well-documented that boys, on average, take longer to master the process. This is because children's bodies develop at different rates, and bladder control develops at its own pace for each child. Starting potty training before a child has developed the physical awareness and control to recognise the need to go often results in frustration for both the parent and the child. The process then becomes drawn out and stressful, whereas waiting until the child is ready makes it far more efficient and less taxing for everyone involved.

The same principle applies to all forms of learning: it is far more effective when the learner is developmentally ready. Take writing as an example. We often overlook physical readiness, such as the development of the bones and muscles in a child's hand, before introducing tasks like holding a pencil or mastering a proper grip. When my daughter was in year five, at around nine or ten years old, she injured her wrist and required an X-ray. The nurse, upon examining the image, initially expressed concern, when she noticed gaps in the hand where certain bones should be. After consulting with a doctor, she realised these gaps were completely normal, as my child's hands were not yet fully developed. This incident was a revelation to me, yet it highlights a critical issue: we often fail to consider whether a child's body is physically ready for tasks like writing when we expect them to develop a pencil grip at the age of four.

For neurodiverse children, these developmental differences can be even more pronounced due to the unique neurological makeup of their brains. Despite this, the education system makes little allowance for such differences, instead forcing all children to conform to the same rigid expectations. This one-size-fits-all approach ignores individual readiness and creates unnecessary challenges, particularly for children whose developmental timelines deviate from the "norm". By failing to accommodate these variations, the system risks hindering both learning and well-being, rather than fostering growth at a pace that suits each child.

The Impact of Trauma on Learning

When children have experienced trauma such as attachment issues, they will often be much closer to the "fight" or "flight" response than children who are neurotypical and who haven't experienced trauma, meaning that their resilience and general feeling of comfort and safety will be lacking, making it much more difficult to make mistakes and learn from them. Therefore, getting to know your learners individually and building up trusting relationships with them will really help when being able to set the right topics and challenges. In general, learners, whether they are neurotypical or neurodiverse will learn best in different ways. Some may be kinaesthetic learners, some auditory, some visual etc. Alistair Smith and Nicola Call's book *The Alps Approach* from the 1990s has some great theories that fit with this idea and they talk about learning styles in detail. In this book they refer to them as "VAK" learning styles which stands for "Visual, auditory and kinesthetic". They prompt teachers to think about how they can boost the probability that all learners can and will be able to access and engage in the learning experience by including activities or resources that help to encourage and support the various learning styles. Whether it be offering opportunities for physical movement, visual inputs or auditory inputs. In so doing this, they believe that this would better imprint the learning that takes place in the lesson into the memory. It has been shown that learning spellings, for example, can be more effective if you include a number of methods to practise them such as tracing them with your finger onto someone's back, using auditory mnemonics or from a visual aspect writing them out in different colours.

Steering Away from a One-Size-Fits-All Approach

If we consider learners as individuals with their own specific needs, it does seem that by teaching in a way that is very uniform and a "one size fits all approach" really isn't ever going to reach all of your learners nor help them reach their full potential. Teachers need to be able to use their skills, knowledge and shared experience to be able to design lessons freely that may not have one specific outcome but that can reach the needs of each child in the class more efficiently. By having a thematic and investigatory approach where the level of challenge is determined by the child themselves with some steering from a teacher who has built a good understanding and secure relationship with that child this could be achieved far more easily and organically rather than a forced mechanical way with a means to meet an already set objective.

Despite advancements in the diagnosis and awareness of Special Educational Needs (SEN) and neurodiversity, significant misunderstandings persist particularly among older generations and those who firmly believe that strict discipline is the only effective way to ensure children learn. For the people who hold this view, this approach often reflects the methods they grew up with and it is what they view as the only way to maintain order and instil life skills. Common phrases often heard from this perspective, such as "They need to learn to conform to get on in the real world", "We shouldn't pander to these children, they need to learn that they can't always have what they want", "It didn't do me any harm", or "They should be made to do the same as everyone else", are rooted in outdated and poorly informed opinions.

Historically, children with SEN were often segregated from mainstream education and, for all intents and purposes, excluded from society, effectively rendered "out of sight, out of mind". While we have moved beyond this exclusionary mindset and now strive for a more inclusive society, this shift requires rethinking some of the traditional approaches that may no longer be effective or appropriate.

Critics may argue that the behaviour and attitudes of younger generations are deteriorating due to a perceived lack of discipline or declining standards. However, it's worth considering whether these challenges stem from outdated methods of managing behaviour that have not evolved alongside modern beliefs and societal attitudes. To truly foster positive change, we must be willing to reconsider our expectations and embrace new approaches to understanding and supporting children's needs, particularly when it comes to managing behaviour. By adapting our methods to align with contemporary understanding, we can create environments that are more inclusive, effective and supportive for all children.

Makaton, Sign Language and Alternative Communication

I have often wondered whether sign language, particularly Makaton, should be incorporated into teacher training and introduced as a statutory requirement in all schools. It sometimes does appear in small quantities, such as signing along to some songs in assemblies or using ACC (Augmentative and Alternative Communication) symbols when giving some instructions, but I mean going the whole hog and integrating some form of sign language into all aspects. As a nation, we are generally quite poor at learning other languages. While schools teach a select few, unless we pursue them at a higher level or move abroad, most of us retain only the basics which lay buried somewhere in the dusty corners of our minds, only to be retrieved when needed for a holiday.

Let's be honest: as English speakers, we often lack the incentive to learn new languages. English is widely spoken around the world, and other nations do an impressive job of learning it. High-quality media, films, television and music, all provide a compelling reason for others to engage with

English. But what if, instead of focusing solely on foreign languages, we placed greater emphasis on learning a form of sign language?

Makaton is a unique language system used in over 40 countries. Unlike British Sign Language (BSL), which is primarily used by the Deaf community. Makaton is designed to support communication for hearing individuals who experience speech difficulties, such as non-verbal autistic people. It combines signs, symbols and spoken words to aid communication. If everyone were proficient in Makaton, society would become far more inclusive, removing barriers for those who struggle with verbal communication while also benefiting kinaesthetic learners who absorb information more effectively through movement.

The incentives for learning Makaton, while perhaps not as immediately compelling as those for English, are undeniable. It would allow us to communicate more effectively with individuals we might otherwise ignore or avoid due to uncertainty about how to interact. It could also provide a meaningful way to engage with babies and toddlers before they develop fluent speech. Imagine the untapped potential of a world where Makaton is simply an ordinary part of how we communicate, woven seamlessly into daily life.

One of the most remarkable aspects of language is its ability to evolve and adapt over time. There is no reason why Makaton could not be integrated into our modern way of communicating, making English even more accessible and universal than it already is.

Reforming the SEND System: A Call for Proficiency and Equity

An effective SEND system relies heavily on robust support systems and collaboration among educators, parents, specialists and the community. Interdisciplinary teams, including speech therapists, occupational therapists and educational psychologists, who play a vital role in developing comprehensive educational plans tailored to each child's needs. Specialists need to be more readily available and affordable so that schools can gain the additional help and support as often and as promptly as needed. For too many children the wait is far too long. Regular training and professional development for teachers on SEND strategies and inclusive practices are essential to ensure that they are well-equipped to support diverse learners.

Advocating for policy reform is crucial in addressing the systemic issues in SEND provision. This includes ensuring adequate funding, reducing bureaucratic hurdles and promoting inclusive education policies that prioritise the needs of neurodiverse learners. Policies should focus on creating flexible curriculums, individualised learning plans and accessible resources that cater to a wide range of learning differences. Schools need to be supported throughout this process by professionals as soon as the school have identified a need. There is so much precious time lost with ever-growing waiting lists leaving children, families and schools without the necessary support for years, in many cases.

Technology can be a powerful tool in supporting SEND learners. Assistive technologies, such as speech-to-text software, assistive writing software such as "Clicker" and interactive learning apps, can all help to provide personalised learning experiences and enhance accessibility. Integrating technology into the classroom not only aids in addressing specific needs but also prepares students for a digital future.

Addressing the needs of SEND learners requires a multifaceted approach that combines understanding, flexibility and innovation. By recognising the unique challenges faced by neurodiverse children and those who have experienced trauma, educators can create more inclusive and effective learning environments. I believe that creating a curriculum that helps to induce a state of "flow" and one which is guided by the interests of the children could have a profound effect on the inclusion of all children, especially those who are neurodiverse. This along with collaboration, advocacy and the strategic use of technology are key to transforming the educational landscape and ensuring that all children can have the opportunity to thrive.

References

Fisher, N. (2023). *A Different Way to Learn*. Jessica Kingsley Publishers.
Kendall, E. (2020). *Helping You to Identify and Understand Autism Masking*. M and R Publishing.
NASEN. (2024, July 1). New data shows increase in SEND to 18.4%. [online] *NASEN*. Available at: https://nasen.org.uk/index.php/news/sen-data-january-2024 [Accessed 17 May 2025].
Smith, A. and Call, N. (1999). *The Alps Approach Accelerated Learning in Primary Schools*. Network Educational Press Ltd.

 Challenging the Doubts

Any significant change will come with doubts about if it is the best course of action to take. With a change such as the ones proposed in this book, I can foresee that there may be fears around the questions, "but are we not just allowing them to do what they want? What will become of behaviour which is already a reportedly significant and growing challenge? Won't it make it worse? What if they choose never to learn to read or write? There may even be fears that this is too liberal or "airy fairy" to work in reality or fears that this won't work with a whole class, especially the large class sizes we have today. There may be scepticism about the actual results and how we could easily measure progress which is able to be compared nationally and globally.

We fear what is different and most of all we fear the unknown. What we do know is what we currently have in place is not working efficiently because there are adults within our society who grow up to be illiterate or have poor literacy skills and, as a consequence, are more likely to be un-employed, in lower paid jobs or even face welfare dependency. The statistics show that a shockingly high percentage of adults in England have not acquired the literacy skills they need leaving them vulnerable in today's society. The national literacy trust claims the following statistics:

> 1 in 6 (18%) of adults in England, or 6.6 million people, can be described as having very poor literacy skills.
>
> (National Literacy Trust, 2017)

Another way to interpret this is that if it is a ratio of 1 in 6, then in every class of 30 we have been failing five children. That does not strike me as a system that is working efficiently.

In the book *Progressively Worse: The Burden of Bad Ideas in British Schools*, Robert Peal (2014) delivers a scathing critique of what he terms "progressive methods". By this he means approaches that prioritise child-centred learning, creativity and a facilitative approach to teaching as opposed to a traditional demonstrator or disseminator of facts. He argues that these strategies have not only failed to improve academic outcomes but have also contributed to declining classroom discipline. According to Peal, where progressive methods have been implemented, they have often replaced direct instruction and subject knowledge, leading to a substantial drop in educational standards.

After reading the book, I found myself questioning whether there might be some misunderstanding surrounding the concept of so-called progressive teaching methods. Specifically, I wondered whether there is a universally accepted definition among educators or if these methods are inherently open to interpretation. Given the ever-evolving nature of education, do teaching professionals maintain a consistent understanding of what constitutes "progressive methods", or does this vary based on context, experience and personal philosophy? The very idea that "progressive methods" could be subject to individual interpretation raises important questions about their practical application and effectiveness in diverse learning environments.

While it is clear that an entirely child-led approach, where children are left to their own devices without any structured guidance, is unlikely to foster optimal learning conditions, the assumption that "progressive methods" are wholly ineffective is overly simplistic. Instead, a balanced approach is essential; one that combines explicit instruction at appropriate levels and time durations with opportunities for hands-on exploration, guided investigations and responsive teaching interventions. When executed thoughtfully, this approach not only strengthens knowledge retention but also nurtures engagement, problem-solving skills and deeper understanding.

A prime example of this effective balance can be seen at Mayflower Primary School in Tower Hamlets, currently (at the time of writing – early 2025) a top-performing state primary school in England. A glance at their curriculum page reveals multiple references to progressive methodologies, including "creative learning", "problem-solving, enquiry and child-led investigations" and "pupils choosing areas of learning that appeal to them". This directly contradicts the notion that "progressive methods" inherently lead to educational decline. Instead, it suggests that their success depends on how they are structured and integrated within a robust teaching framework.

A review that can be found on the Libertarian Education website, delves into an analysis of Robert Peal's book. In the writer's reflections they point out some possible "cherry picking" of information to back up Robert Peal's evidently rigid view of how there really is no worthy benefit to progressive methods which is often portrayed in the book as letting the children do what they want. The writer, Hansen (2015), picks up on and challenges the points made in the book about Summerhill's GCSE results which are portrayed in a "negative light". The writer highlights the following point:

> that it is the only year of Summerhill's GCSE results reported in this book. The school has often exceeded national averages in the past- and all, I repeat, while giving the kids freedom to do what they like and not bother going to lessons if they don't want to.
>
> (Hansen, 2015)

Reading this somewhat flattened Robert Peal's whole argument for me. I felt that, overall, he had not really understood "progressive methods" in the same way that I do or how I believe they should be implemented in the classroom. To me, "progressive methods" are those grounded in scientific research and our growing understanding of how children learn. They are responsive to the changing needs of society and the learners within it. Clinging rigidly to traditional approaches, under the assumption that older methods are inherently better, is not forward thinking, nor is it supported by the evolving evidence base around effective teaching and learning.

Based on both research and real-world examples, it is not the use of "progressive methods" that determines educational effectiveness but rather the way in which they are executed. When balanced thoughtfully with structured teaching, they can create a dynamic and highly effective learning environment, rather than contributing to the decline that Peal suggests.

Child-Led Learning – How Will They Learn to Read?

Let's address the concern that a more child-led curriculum might hinder the acquisition of essential skills such as reading, writing and arithmetic. How can we ensure that children do not develop gaps in their learning that may hold them back?

Firstly, it is important to point out that what I am proposing is not an absence of teaching. Humans are not born with knowledge, they need to acquire it. It has more to do with the way in which this is done. Neither does it mean that teachers should have lower expectations – in fact the opposite is true. It is about enabling the right environment to nurture happy, confident children who are able to be receptive to learning. It is important to recognise that our current curriculum and education system do not entirely prevent learning gaps. There are still individuals who reach adulthood struggling with literacy, as mentioned earlier. This raises an important question: could a more child-led approach actually help tackle this issue? I believe it can.

When a child takes the lead in their own learning, they naturally encounter the need to develop specific skills to achieve their desired outcomes. They learn because they want to, because they have a clear purpose and because they are engaged in meaningful tasks. This intrinsic motivation allows learning to be more effective and long-lasting. In contrast, when children are required to learn through monotonous, uninspiring tasks with no clear relevance, the process becomes significantly more challenging and time-consuming.

The role of the teacher, therefore, becomes one of careful and strategic planning. Teachers must provide resources and opportunities that align with students' interests while also ensuring that fundamental skills are embedded within these activities. For instance, some may worry that children who struggle with reading, such as those with dyslexia, might avoid reading altogether if given too much autonomy. However, children often resist reading because their experiences with it have been largely negative such as being forced to read uninspiring texts or being made to read aloud in uncomfortable settings. By allowing more autonomy and providing appropriate support, for example, coloured overlays, text-to-speech technology, or structured guidance, we can foster a more positive and encouraging learning environment.

Many believe that the introduction of phonics instruction has revolutionised literacy education, with programmes like "Little Wandle" gaining popularity due to their structured, repetitive approaches. While phonics instruction has certainly yielded positive outcomes, it should not be viewed as the sole method for teaching reading. Phonics is a crucial component, but reading proficiency also requires the integration of multiple strategies, including contextual awareness, sight recognition and comprehension skills.

For example, take the word "read". Without context, there is no way to determine whether it should be pronounced as "r-e-d" (past tense) or "r-ee-d" (present tense). Additionally, some words defy phonetic decoding entirely such as "Wednesday", "lettuce", "receipt" or "biscuit". This demonstrates why a balanced approach to reading instruction is necessary, incorporating phonics alongside exposure to a wide variety of texts and reading experiences. Reading is better taught through reading 1-1 with a child, where the child has been able to make their own choice about the reading material, therefore adding in a child-led element.

Ultimately, phonics should remain a key part of the curriculum, but it should be taught within a context that makes learning meaningful and engaging. By embedding reading instruction within children's interests, we can nurture a lifelong love of reading rather than reducing it to a mere functional necessity. A child-led approach, when thoughtfully implemented, has the potential to make learning more effective, enjoyable and enduring.

An Evolution in Inclusivity

Our society has undergone significant shifts in values and principles, reflecting a steady evolution towards greater acceptance and inclusivity. We are growing in our understanding and tolerance of differences be it cultural, racial, religious, or related to disabilities. Today, we strive to empower individuals to have a voice where, in the past, they may have been silenced or just simply not been given the opportunity because it was not deemed to be relevant. We actively seek out and celebrate inspiring examples, from the achievements of Paralympians to the courage of historical figures like Rosa Parks, fostering positivity and resilience in future generations.

By learning from the experiences of others throughout history, we are consciously choosing to create a more inclusive society. As societal values evolve, our systems and processes must also adapt to sustain this progress and build a foundation for a better future. This is evident in numerous examples of systemic change. In terms of education, we have seen many changes but perhaps one of the starkest shifts would be the movement away from harsh disciplinary measures such as caning or public shaming (e.g. the "dunce cap") to fostering more inclusive, compassionate and understanding environments. Other significant examples of social changes and advancements, to my mind, include women's rights and how they have advanced dramatically, moving from a time when women were denied the right to vote or participate in public life to the implementation of equality legislation and their active involvement in all areas of society. There have been many advancements in the medical profession but when we consider mental health treatment, it has evolved from practices of institutionalisation and harmful interventions like forced lobotomies to community-based support, medication and therapies that prioritise dignity and recovery. In the past, the law and justice system relied on brutal punishments such as hanging, torture and mutilation. Today, the focus has shifted towards rehabilitation and restorative justice. All of these examples show an evolution of deepening understanding of each other leading to tolerance and growing kindness.

While we have made significant strides, the journey is far from over. There is still work to be done to ensure that inclusivity becomes ingrained in all aspects of society. By reflecting on what we've learned and applying these lessons, we can continue to pave the way towards a more equitable and inclusive future. A future where every individual has the opportunity to thrive and develop a lifelong love of learning. Ultimately, the need to continue to move forwards is why change is necessary and seemingly overdue in terms of our current education system.

Tackling Challenging Behaviours

Behaviour is often a key issue in discussions about teacher retention. The prevailing perception is that teachers are increasingly faced with challenging behaviour from pupils across all age groups. Dealing with violent or threatening behaviour creates an environment that is far from conducive to effective learning. However, it is not just these high-level incidents that cause concern. Persistent low-level disruptions such as answering back, refusing to complete work, ignoring instructions, making disruptive comments or noises and calling out contribute to a broader sense of declining pupil behaviour over time.

Many attribute this decline to a lack of discipline, but it is important to consider what we truly mean by that. Corporal punishment has rightly been abandoned, replaced by consequence-based systems such as loss of break time, time-out, removal from class and parental involvement. In more serious cases, schools may resort to suspensions or even permanent exclusion. More recently, many schools have adopted restorative practices, which focus on equipping pupils with the tools to resolve conflicts, repair harm and build positive relationships. Research, such as the Learning Policy Institute's report *Fostering Belonging, Transforming Schools: The Impact of Restorative Practices* (2023), highlights the effectiveness of this approach in reducing school exclusions.

Referring back to Robert Peal's book *Progressively Worse: The Burden of Bad Ideas in British Schools* he describes an account of a teacher in a secondary school who claims he was bullied by a thirteen-year-old child that he had regular contact with. The bullying became increasingly problematic as time went on until the teacher feared for his own safety. This is a troubling story but I am unconvinced that this is a result of "progressive methods" but rather the absence of methods entirely to address this worrying scenario, namely when the poor teacher in this situation approached senior staff for help nothing was done. Robert Peal blames this on the "permissive philosophy" of some head teachers meaning that they are neglecting their duty to enforce discipline. But could he be overlooking the difference here between taking no action against addressing unwanted behaviours and implementing alternative methods such as "restorative practices"?

In terms of discipline involving stricter rules and sanctions – what could this actually look like? It is clear that the behaviour, in the above example, was unacceptable and could not continue in this way and that ensuring that the rules are clearly laid out to the pupil would be essential to ensuring that he knew and understood the expectations. A clear set of steps that would happen if these rules are not followed could then be put into motion ultimately resulting in a sanction appropriate and in proportion to the breaking of the rule. Traditionally this may involve,

- a reprimand
- confiscating an item from the child which may have been a distraction.
- a letter to parents or carers
- removal from a class or group
- loss of privileges
- suspension
- exclusion

In the case described, it had almost certainly reached a point of suspension if not exclusion as the situation had been left to escalate. This provides a solution for the teacher, the other pupils who were being disrupted and the

Challenging the Doubts

wider school community but what it does not do is fix the problem for the offending child, it merely bats the problem away, out of sight out of mind, meanwhile the damage that it does to a child who is evidently in dire need of help and guidance is left in a vulnerable and hopeless situation.

To me there are many unanswered questions to the example that Robert Peal gives that would help to gain a clearer understanding of how this situation came to be. The questions that spring immediately to mind are:

- Did this same child behave in this way towards other staff and if so how did they deal with it?
- Were there any notable triggers for this behaviour?
- Was there a pattern to the behaviours?
- We are informed that the teacher approached senior staff about the behaviour but had any other strategies been tried?
- What do we know about the pupil's background?

These are all important questions to begin to unpick the behaviour and work to find a solution to fix it. In this case, a number of things needed to happen. As soon as the behaviour began, it should have been addressed with the pupil. In the described scenario, without knowing the finer details, it is reasonable to assume that this behaviour was an example of seeking power through a display of aggression, which could be the result of unresolved trauma. Therefore, addressing the behaviour with the pupil needs to be done in a skilled manner, and may be better coming from another member of staff who is not directly involved. The following steps could be taken:

- Reminding the pupil of the rules and expectations is the first port of call, ensuring they have a clear understanding of them.
- Take restorative action, where a meeting takes place between the pupil and teacher with another member of staff present. Ensure the pupil has an understanding of the consequences of their actions (both natural, i.e. disruption to learning and enforced, e.g. loss of break time) and that they have an understanding of what the next steps will be if the behaviour continues, for example, removal from class, parents called etc.
- Establishing the root cause (aggression often masks underlying issues such as insecurity, frustration, or unmet needs) which can only be done through talking to the pupil and building a trusting relationship. It may be that this pupil requires behaviour support in order to develop an

understanding of the consequences this behaviour has on himself and others as well as some targeted work on communication and respect.
- Working to build a positive relationship so that mutual respect can be gained. (Hard to do when you feel personally attacked but essential nonetheless). For this you need to look hard for the positive and point it out as soon as it is noted. Emphasise their strengths, pointing out that you can see their potential and helping them to redirect their need for power into more constructive channels. You can even try engaging them in leadership type roles highlighting that you have noticed their confidence and determination and would love to see it channelled in a positive direction.
- In this particular case, it may have been necessary for a senior member of staff to observe, model, help redirect and even arrange for some team teaching to take place to fully support the teacher who, in the end, could not see any other way out of the situation than to leave.

Throughout my career, I have observed a wide range of behaviour management styles. Some teachers, often informally described as "old school", adopt a strict approach that keeps pupils in line through authority and discipline. While this may create order initially, it can also foster a fear of making mistakes, ultimately hindering learning, as mistakes are essential to the learning process. Additionally, a rigid, authoritarian approach can make it difficult to build positive relationships with pupils, which are crucial for fostering mutual respect.

There is a fundamental difference between a child behaving out of fear and one behaving out of respect for a teacher they trust. A child needs to feel listened to, understood and valued. This is especially true for those with attachment difficulties, for whom trust must be carefully built. Without this foundation, achieving genuine mutual respect (and, by extension, a positive learning environment) becomes much more difficult.

In the past, behaviour was often seen as something to be quashed. Phrases like "stamped out" come to mind. While it is true that, for society to function, we must all learn that certain behaviours are unacceptable and that our actions should not negatively impact others, it is equally important to recognise that all behaviour is a form of communication.

Behaviour is not just about what we see; it is about the underlying reasons that lead to those actions. Children express their needs, emotions and responses to their environment through their behaviour. The way they do this varies greatly depending on their emotional and cognitive development, particularly for those who may not yet have the language or self-awareness to articulate how they feel. Just as we use words to communicate, behaviour can be a non-verbal expression of an unmet need, frustration, anxiety, or even a desire for connection.

A common phrase often heard when it comes to misbehaviour is, "Oh, they're just attention-seeking – ignore them". While ignoring a child may eventually stop the behaviour in the moment, it does not address the underlying need. That child will continue seeking attention, often resorting to negative behaviours because, for them, any attention is better than none. A more effective approach would be to proactively meet that need in a structured way – perhaps by timetabling one-on-one time with a teaching assistant to play a game or engage in a meaningful activity. By providing positive attention in a controlled way, we reduce the likelihood of attention-seeking behaviours manifesting disruptively in the classroom.

Similarly, a child who frequently calls out in class may not be seeking attention at all, they might be looking for reassurance or struggling with impulse control. Rather than focusing solely on stopping the behaviour, it is more effective to explore what support could be put in place to help them develop self-regulation skills. This might involve trial and error with different strategies, but ultimately, addressing the root cause is more beneficial than simply trying to enforce compliance.

Other common behaviours, such as refusing to complete work, are often misinterpreted as defiance. However, a child who resists a task may actually be struggling with the content, feeling overwhelmed, or lacking confidence. Likewise, a student who becomes physically aggressive (or one who withdraws completely, hiding under a table and refusing to engage) may not be *choosing* to misbehave. Instead, they could be reacting to stress, trauma, or an inability to regulate their emotions. Recognising these underlying causes allows us to implement long-term solutions that address the root issues, rather than applying short-term fixes that may ultimately escalate the behaviour over time.

By viewing behaviour as communication, educators can shift their focus from asking, "How do I stop this behaviour?" to "What is this behaviour telling me?" This perspective fosters a more empathetic and proactive approach, helping to support children effectively by addressing the causes of their behaviour rather than just the symptoms.

Rather than focusing on *controlling* pupil behaviour, it is more effective to think about *enabling* children to make considerate and appropriate choices while ensuring their needs are met. Achieving this often requires compromise and, most importantly, the development of positive relationships.

Confrontational approaches should be avoided at all costs, as they quickly turn into a battle of wills. When an adult engages in a power struggle with a child, it becomes easy to lose control of both their emotions and the situation itself. A child will instinctively pick up on this loss of control, which can make them feel emotionally unsafe and increase the likelihood of their behaviour escalating.

Remaining calm in such moments is a skill that takes practice. As humans, we naturally react to what others say, and it is easy to perceive challenging behaviour as a personal attack. However, shifting our mindset to view behaviour as a symptom of an underlying issue helps to remove personal emotion from the equation. Instead of reacting defensively, we can think, "This behaviour is communicating an unmet need – let's try to understand what's behind it". Addressing the root causes of behaviour leads to more effective, long-term solutions, helping pupils to develop self-reflection and emotional regulation skills.

It is also essential for senior staff to involve all relevant staff members when managing challenging behaviour. Too often, I have seen teachers express frustration when a child sent out of class for disruptive behaviour returns after what appears to be nothing more than a chat and a biscuit with a senior member of staff. From the teacher's perspective, this can feel like their exhaustion and efforts to manage the situation have been disregarded and they may very well feel undermined. However, if we consider the possible reasoning behind this response, we might find that the senior leader identified an unmet need – perhaps the child had not eaten breakfast that morning and was struggling to focus as a result. In this case, providing a biscuit was not a reward for poor behaviour, but a necessary intervention to help the child re-engage in learning.

This highlights the importance of clear communication between all parties involved in behaviour management. Staff must understand not only the actions taken but also the reasons behind them to maintain a consistent and supportive approach. This does not mean there should be no consequences for poor behaviour, but rather that consequences should be framed in a way that helps children understand the natural outcomes of their choices. Wherever possible, a restorative approach should be used, focusing on helping pupils reflect on their actions and repair any harm caused, rather than simply enforcing punitive measures.

Having clear boundaries is essential in helping children feel safe, and communicating these effectively is key. It is equally important to ensure that any expectations and boundaries we set are developmentally appropriate. For example, we cannot expect Reception-aged children to sit and engage in a carpet session for extended periods without losing focus. Most children at that stage simply do not have the capacity for sustained attention. According to the *Ready Kids Occupational Therapy* website, the average attention span for a child in Reception is 5–10 minutes, whereas a Year 6 child can typically focus for 20–30 minutes.

> Here, the general rule of thumb is that a child should have an attention span for 2–3 minutes per year of the child's age. That's the time span for which a typical child can maintain their focus on a particular task or activity.
>
> (Shakibaie, 2021)

Of course, this is only an average. Some children may struggle to focus for as long as their peers. This variation must be considered when setting behaviour expectations. If a child begins to fidget on the carpet after five minutes, it is likely they have reached their limit, and punishing them for this would be unfair. Instead, we should consider strategies such as incorporating movement breaks or shortening the input time. Rather than viewing the child's behaviour as disruptive, we should reflect on whether our expectations are realistic. Supporting children in ways that align with their developmental needs is crucial for their well-being and future engagement in learning.

Shifting towards a more child-led curriculum and carefully designing lessons to create opportunities for "flow" can significantly reduce behaviour challenges in the classroom. When children are deeply engaged in purposeful learning, their focus remains on the task at hand, minimising off-task behaviours that often lead to low-level disruptions.

Engineering opportunities for "flow" naturally invites collaboration, helping children develop teamwork skills, strengthen relationships and build mutual respect and understanding. As educators observe and guide learning, they can step in to support students when needed, helping them navigate challenges and develop problem-solving skills. While restorative practices remain essential, proactive strategies that diffuse tensions and support children in resolving difficulties before escalation are even more effective.

Creating the right environment and learning opportunities not only enhances student engagement but also allows teachers to take on a more facilitative role. Instead of constantly managing behaviour, educators can focus on guiding discussions, demonstrating key concepts and asking thoughtful questions that encourage critical thinking, in turn helping children make informed choices and take ownership of their learning. It is about shifting our position in terms of managing behaviour to thinking and acting proactively ultimately reducing the need to act reactively.

Essentially, children learn to behave well because they recognise the benefits it brings them, rather than simply following rules without understanding the reasons behind them. When they experience positive outcomes, whether it be stronger relationships, a sense of achievement, or a more enjoyable learning environment, they are more likely to make considerate choices independently, rather than just complying with instructions.

Most children naturally want to please an adult with whom they have formed a positive relationship and respond well to praise. They also tend to focus on what the adult draws attention to. If a teacher consistently highlights low-level disruptive behaviours, they may find themselves in a cycle of negative reinforcement. However, by focusing on positive behaviours instead, teachers can create a more constructive learning environment.

For example, if Child A is exhibiting low-level disruptive behaviours while Child B is following instructions and sitting attentively, the teacher can choose to acknowledge Child B instead: "Well done, Child B! You are sitting still and looking in my direction just as I asked". This not only reinforces Child B's positive behaviour but also provides Child A with a clear model of expectations. As soon as Child A adjusts their behaviour accordingly, they should also receive praise, reinforcing their positive choices.

In my experience, when children entered the classroom unsettled after break time, pointing out and praising those who were displaying the desired behaviours encouraged the rest to follow suit. Ultimately, we get more of what we pay attention to. Positive reinforcement is essential in helping children understand rules and expectations.

This principle extends beyond the classroom. As adults, we perform best in our jobs when we know our efforts will be recognised whether through natural outcomes, pay rises, special awards, or other forms of acknowledgement. Similarly, in dog training, ignoring unwanted behaviours while immediately praising desired ones, conditions the dog to behave appropriately. This demonstrates the power of praise in shaping and nurturing the behaviours we want to see, making it a crucial tool in teaching and guidance. And, in my opinion, all the more powerful than a good telling off or picking out the negatives.

Balancing Structure and Freedom in the School Day

With more of a leaning towards a child-led learning approach, some may be concerned about a lack of structure or even a lack of rules and expectations. However, a child-led approach does not mean removing rules, expectations, or structure. Instead, it involves engaging children more actively in these processes. Structure and consistency become even more important in ensuring clarity, understanding and fair implementation of expectations.

Regarding the structure of the school day, we often limit ourselves by trying to fit in an overwhelming number of initiatives, interventions and requirements. If teachers were granted greater flexibility to adapt their approach based on the immediate needs of their students, the learning experience could become far more effective for children and significantly less pressured for teachers.

For instance, timetabled sessions for subjects like PSHCE (Personal, Social, Health and Citizenship Education) are undoubtedly valuable, but teaching such topics in context, when relevant situations arise, can be far more impactful. I recall a lesson on bullying where I used two apples to demonstrate the power of words. One apple had been deliberately dropped before the session, while the other remained untouched. The students took turns saying unkind words to the bruised apple and kind words to the untouched one. When I cut the apples open, they saw the bruising inside the first apple, illustrating that words can cause unseen harm. While the lesson was effective, I couldn't help but think how much more powerful it would have been if it had directly related to a real-life situation within the class. Addressing such issues at the moment they occur allows children to make stronger, more personal connections to the lesson, reinforcing the intended message in a meaningful way.

Structure to the school day is important because it provides children with security and stability, but we need to take the "Goldilocks" approach by introducing just the right amount. Not too much so that it becomes restrictive and limits learning outcomes, but just enough to provide guidance and consistency. A flexible structure allows children to feel safe and supported while also giving them the freedom to explore and engage in meaningful learning experiences. Striking this balance ensures that children thrive academically, socially and emotionally in a way that fosters both independence and a strong sense of responsibility.

It is also important to minimise the number of transitions between activities throughout the school day to allow a state of "flow" to occur. Frequent shifts from one task to another disrupt children's focus and make it difficult for them to fully engage in deeper learning experiences. When transitions are reduced, children have more uninterrupted time to immerse themselves in activities, fostering greater concentration, creativity and productivity. Therefore, there is a clear advantage to be gained from reducing the timetable which is easier to do if we remember that subjects can be intertwined and do not have to be stand-alone.

We also need to be mindful of transitions throughout the school day. Too often, we expect children to move abruptly from one unfamiliar challenge to another without adequate preparation. Given that it is human nature to fear the unknown, this can be particularly anxiety-inducing for children, especially those who are naturally more anxious. As adults, when faced with a new experience, such as attending a work-related course, we take steps to prepare ourselves. We might research the location on "Google Street View", plan our travel route and review the agenda beforehand. These small preparations help us feel more comfortable and confident. Similarly, we cannot expect children to seamlessly adapt to new situations without support. Tools such as social stories, task boards and visual timetables can significantly reduce uncertainty, providing children with a clearer sense of what to expect and easing transitions in a way that minimises stress and maximises engagement.

Going back to the point made in the earlier chapter "Special Educational Needs and Disabilities" about the institutionalisation that pupils must fall into, in order that they "tow-the-line" and follow the rules can in effect remove some of the learning opportunities for children to experience real-life consequences and learn from them. We looked at the example of school uniform and how the consequence for not wearing it would be imposed by the school, that is, there is no natural negative consequence for not wearing a uniform, merely an imposed one. Nothing bad will spontaneously happen and therefore the school must create a sanction. There are lots of examples like this that fundamentally feed into the functionality of our current school systems. However, if we look at this from a different perspective what we see is that we may actually be doing our pupils a disservice by removing the opportunities to develop assertiveness over passivity and compliance.

The current approach prioritises rule-following over fostering a deeper understanding of the reasons behind those rules or the impact of one's actions. As a result, children may learn to associate behaviour with imposed consequences rather than developing the ability to self-regulate or reflect on how their choices affect others and their environment.

This reliance on extrinsic motivators can undermine opportunities for children to learn from natural consequences, which are often far more effective in shaping behaviour and building critical thinking skills. For example, if a child disrupts a group activity, the natural consequence might be difficulty completing the task leading to embarrassment or frustration among peers. After all, real-life experiences carry meaningful lessons. In contrast, a prescribed punishment like losing break time might fail to connect the behaviour with its actual impact, leaving the child focused on the penalty rather than the learning opportunity.

By encouraging obedience at the expense of intrinsic motivation, schools risk stifling children's ability to think critically, make independent decisions and develop a genuine sense of accountability, all of which are skills that are essential for their growth and success beyond the classroom.

Crowded Classrooms, Shrinking Support

In our modern times, an increasing population has led to growing class sizes in primary schools. Compounding this issue, financial constraints have resulted in funding cuts, particularly affecting the number of teaching assistants. Once a common presence in classrooms, full-time general teaching assistants are now a rarity unless working lower down the school where it is important to meet the ratio requirements or working as one-on-one support with a SEND child. This shift has placed greater demands on teachers, who must cater to larger numbers of pupils while managing the limitations of classroom space and resources.

One of the biggest questions arising from this challenge is whether a child-led learning approach is still viable in a classroom of, say, 35 children. The answer, while complex, highlights both the difficulties and the unique advantages of such an approach.

Managing a large class presents numerous difficulties. Close monitoring of each child's learning process becomes more challenging, particularly when children have diverse abilities, learning styles and individual needs. Teachers may feel pressured to deliver whole-class instruction to ensure content is covered efficiently, yet this traditional model often does not cater to the varying paces at which children learn. The temptation to rely on structured, worksheet-based activities may grow, as they offer a straightforward means of assessment, but these can limit deeper thinking, collaboration and creative problem-solving.

Furthermore, teachers may feel an urge to intervene frequently, guiding children step by step to ensure they grasp key concepts. While this is often well-intentioned, it can sometimes hinder a child's natural problem-solving abilities and autonomy. Reflecting on my own school experience, I remember feeling frustrated when a teacher stood over me, offering guidance before I had the chance to explore solutions myself. This highlights the importance of balancing support with trust and simply giving children space to try, fail and self-correct before stepping in.

Despite these challenges, a child-led learning approach offers significant benefits that can help children to thrive, even in a larger class. One of its greatest strengths is that it encourages children to self-differentiate, meaning they naturally engage with tasks at their own level – reducing a teacher's workload. When children take ownership of their learning, they build independence, resilience and problem-solving skills. Instead of constant direct instruction, the teacher shifts into the role of an observer and facilitator – stepping in to scaffold learning when needed, but also knowing when to hold back and let discovery unfold.

Peer interaction becomes a powerful tool, allowing students to share different perspectives, challenge each other's thinking and develop social and communication skills. In contrast, if the majority of lessons consist of closed-ended, worksheet-based tasks, opportunities for discussion, debate and creative problem-solving are lost. It is vital that children learn how to engage in collaborative, constructive conversations – skills that are essential not just in school, but in life.

While it is undeniable that larger class sizes and fewer support staff present difficulties, the potential benefits of a well-implemented child-led approach are hard to ignore. Rather than seeing large classes as a barrier, we can view them as an opportunity to foster independence, collaboration and critical thinking. Not to mention lessen the workload on teachers.

With thoughtful planning and skilled facilitation, teachers can create dynamic learning environments where children feel empowered to explore, question and engage meaningfully with their learning.

Ultimately, the key is balance. We need to understand when to step in and when to step back, creating space for children to develop independence while providing the right level of support. By shifting the focus from constant direct instruction to observation and timely intervention, we equip children with the confidence and skills to become lifelong learners.

Data and Measuring Performance

One of the most contentious issues lies in obtaining "statistical data", often used by governments to showcase their successes while in power. Statistical data is typically favoured over anecdotal evidence because it can be manipulated and presented in ways that cast a more favourable light. For example, the Government recently announced that England had risen in global maths rankings, moving from 17th to 11th place. However, a closer examination of the data revealed a different story. England's performance had actually declined compared to previous years, but the drop was less severe than that of other countries – an important nuance that was conveniently overlooked.

The official report referenced by the DFE (Department for Education) even acknowledges this:

> England's score of 492 was significantly lower than the 504 achieved in 2018, although it was not significantly different to average scores in PISA cycles prior to 2018.
>
> (Ingram et al., 2023, p. 10)

This example underscores how data can be framed to create an illusion of progress when, in reality, there has been no significant improvement.

Moreover, the accuracy of such international comparisons is questionable. Children across the world do not take identical tests, as logistical challenges make this impossible. Instead, comparisons are based on standardised assessments, such as PISA, which focus primarily on reading, writing and maths. Therefore, these assessments do not account for the overall effectiveness of each country's education system when you consider subjects outside of these.

School systems, funding levels, pupil selection processes and cultural and societal factors vary greatly between countries, making it difficult to draw meaningful comparisons. Such differences introduce significant challenges to the accuracy and relevance of these rankings, ultimately limiting their usefulness as a measure of educational success.

We will explore assessment in more detail in a later chapter, but it is already clear that, despite the education system's heavy reliance on formal assessments, the current approach is deeply flawed. There must be a better way!

References

Darling-Hammond, S. (2023). *Fostering Belonging, Transforming Schools: The Impact of Restorative Practices*. Learning Policy Institute. Available at: https://learningpolicyinstitute.org/product/impact-restorative-practices-report [Accessed 5 June 2025]. https://doi.org/10.54300/169.703.

Hansen, D. (2015, April 1). *Progressively worse*. [online] Libed.org.uk. Available at: https://www.libed.org.uk/index.php/articles/510-progressively-worse [Accessed 17 May 2025].

Ingram, J., Stiff, J., Cadwallader, S., Lee, G. and Kayton, H. (2023). *PISA 2022: National report for England*. [online] Available at: https://assets.publishing.service.gov.uk/media/656dc3321104cf0013fa742f/PISA_2022_England_National_Report.pdf [Accessed 5 June 2025].

Mayflower Primary School (2025). *Curriculum*. [online] Mayflower Primary School. Available at: https://www.mayflower.towerhamlets.sch.uk/curriculum [Accessed 17 Mar. 2025].

National Literacy Trust (2017). *What is literacy?* [online] National Literacy Trust. Available at: https://literacytrust.org.uk/information/what-is-literacy/ [Accessed 5 June 2025].

Peal, R. (2014). *Progressively Worse: The Burden of Bad Ideas in British Schools*. Civitas, Institute for the Study of Civil Society.

Shakibaie, S. (2021). Child's average attention span by age: From toddler to teens. [online] *Ready Kids*. Available at: https://readykids.com.au/average-attention-span-by-age/#elementor-toc__heading-anchor-3 [Accessed 5 June 2025].

Rethinking Homework for Engagement and "Flow"

The very word *homework* often elicits a groan and this is not just from students, but from parents as well. But why does it carry such a sense of dread? What is it about homework that makes it feel like a burden rather than a meaningful extension of learning?

One of the key challenges with homework is that home is fundamentally different from school. Home is a space where children can unwind, be themselves and engage in activities of their own choosing rather than following structured instruction. By assigning homework, teachers blur the boundary between school and home, introducing an additional demand into a child's personal time and space.

While some forms of homework, such as regular reading, have been shown to support learning and long-term progress, excessive, poorly designed or repetitive assignments can have the opposite effect. They can lead to stress, burnout and a growing resistance to learning. For younger children, in particular, homework can take away valuable time for play-based learning, which is essential for cognitive, social and emotional development.

For many parents, the mere mention of homework can turn into a battleground, particularly if it triggers anxiety in their child. Striking the right balance between offering support and unintentionally taking over can be a difficult and murky area. Parents want to help, but too much involvement can undermine the purpose of the task, while too little can leave children feeling lost or unsupported.

In recent years, project-based homework has become increasingly popular in primary schools. Instead of weekly worksheets, children are given a term to complete a selection of activities related to their topic, allowing for more creativity, autonomy and flexibility. From a child's perspective, this approach often feels less pressured, as they have more time and freedom to complete tasks in a way that suits them. However, in my experience, these projects can sometimes evolve into an unspoken competition among parents, that is, who can build the most impressive model or create the most polished presentation? In many cases, the work becomes more reflective of the parent's efforts than the child's learning, defeating the purpose of independent study.

Another growing concern with modern homework is the increasing reliance on screen-based tasks. Many schools now set spellings, times tables and other core skills through online platforms or apps. While these tools can be engaging and effective, they also present a challenge for families trying to limit screen time at home. Parents who want to encourage offline activities may feel conflicted when homework requires additional screen use, particularly after a school day that may have already involved interactive whiteboards or tablet-based learning. It also raises issues of accessibility and digital equity as not all families have equal access to technology or a quiet space for online learning, potentially putting some children at a disadvantage.

Ultimately, if homework is to be given, it should be appropriate, meaningful and designed to be completed independently. Parents should play a supportive, rather than directive role in helping to establish routines, offering encouragement and maintaining communication with teachers without feeling the pressure to complete the work for their child.

There are, of course, exceptions such as moments when children take the initiative to work on something at home and eagerly bring it in to share with their teacher. Interestingly, in my experience, these pieces of work are rarely the result of assigned homework. Instead, they tend to be personal projects sparked by genuine curiosity or inspiration.

For example, a child might bring in an object they have found or acquired that links to the class topic (I once had a child bring in a badger skull they had found on a walk), or perhaps a story they have written based on their favourite cartoon character. Some children might create a detailed write-up with photos from a museum visit or a family trip that connects to their class topic, such as a castle visit after studying medieval history or a nature journal documenting wildlife in their garden after a science lesson on habitats. Others may take a maths concept learned in school and apply it in a real-world context – for example, measuring ingredients for baking or constructing something with precise measurements at home.

Rethinking Homework for Engagement and "Flow"

The key distinction here is between homework that is "set" and expected by a deadline versus work that emerges organically from a child's own interest and enthusiasm. When children are captivated in the moment, they experience "flow" and that state of deep engagement is where learning feels effortless and enjoyable. Rather than completing a task because they *have to*, they are driven by curiosity and passion, which leads to deeper learning and a greater sense of accomplishment.

This raises an important question: how can schools foster an environment where more children feel inspired to extend their learning beyond the classroom, not because they are told to, but because they *want* to?

I will never forget my time in a year 3 class when I worked with a group of three boys who had been unofficially labelled as *troublesome*. They were classic examples of reluctant learners and were caught in a negative cycle where they constantly sought attention, even if it was for the wrong reasons. More often than not, that attention came in the form of reprimands, reinforcing their reputation rather than breaking the pattern.

At the time, I was working as a teaching assistant – a role that, having previously been a teacher, gave me a completely different perspective. It allowed me to step back, observe the *whole* classroom dynamic, and, most importantly, gave me the time and space to build meaningful relationships with the children.

One particular lesson stands out. The class had been working on division using the *chunking* method, and these three boys were visibly struggling with the concept. Their frustration would quickly turn into disruptive behaviour, and it was clear that they would eventually disengage entirely without support. I was asked to take them out of the classroom for some one-on-one support in a spare room. Predictably, they seemed to *enjoy* being sent out – it was a familiar routine for them, a way of gaining attention even if it was for negative reasons.

From the moment we started, they tested the boundaries, pushing buttons to see how I would react. I made a conscious decision to ignore low-level disruptive behaviours and instead focus only on acknowledging and reinforcing positive behaviours. Bit by bit, their resistance softened. Praise worked wonders. As the lesson progressed, I could see their confidence growing, and by the end, they were visibly proud of what they had achieved.

But what happened next surprised me the most. As we were finishing up, all three of them asked for more work to take home. I have to admit, I was taken aback, but I gladly gave them some extra practice. The next morning, they came into class, beaming with pride, clutching the work they had completed independently at home.

It was a powerful moment and one that has stayed with me ever since. It reinforced just how transformative positive reinforcement can be, especially for children who exhibit challenging behaviour. When we shift the focus from discipline to encouragement, when we find ways to *ignite* a spark of enthusiasm rather than simply managing behaviour, the impact can be profound. It was a reminder that every child *wants* to succeed – they just need to believe they can.

Do the pros outweigh the cons when it comes to teachers dishing out homework? It would appear that it depends on the quality and quantity of homework given. I would argue that limiting "set" homework and encouraging child-initiated activity at home, particularly for those of primary age would be more beneficial to their overall development not forgetting that engaging in play is crucial for a child's brain development and unless a child is in reception or year one generally they are not given enough time in the school day to "play". Sharing books at home does show lots of benefits including helping to develop a lifelong love of reading, developing vocabulary and language skills and overall better learning outcomes, but it is important that the child has autonomy over the choice of text and is not "made" to read a text that they do not enjoy as this can have the opposite effect. When I was young, I remember having to read the One, Two, Three and Away series of books which included characters such as Billy Blue Hat, Roger Red Hat and Jennifer Yellow Hat. Many people will remember the Biff, Chip and Kipper books from the Oxford Reading Tree. More recently, reading books that link closely with phonics schemes are tending to be used. Although these books are great in the sense that they are carefully written to build up reading skills, they are not always terribly inspiring or exciting. I personally remember finding the One, Two, Three and Away series a bit of a chore. I did however enjoy the Puddle Lane books and was lucky enough to be brought up surrounded by books and to have frequent trips to the local library – something that is sadly becoming increasingly rare in our modern society. The key is having access to a choice of quality reading materials that children can freely access. A good sized and good quality school library is one way to do this but sadly not all schools have a library. A survey conducted by the national literacy trust in 2022 found that

> 1 in 7 state primary schools do not have a dedicated library space which impacts educational outcomes and the greater wellbeing of over 750,000 children in the UK
>
> (National Literacy Trust, 2022)

While reading at home or at least having the opportunities to read and share books at home does appear to have a positive impact on children's learning outcomes it isn't clear how much of an impact other forms of homework have overall because there are many changing factors involved. I think what is clear though, is that if it becomes a huge battle at home and both parents and children become stressed by it, then really it becomes counterproductive.

Extracurricular Activities and Equal Opportunities

With such a large amount of emphasis being put on the core subjects in schools, and with time constantly being squeezed by one incentive or another, I think it is important that children have time to explore other hobbies or interests too such as sports, arts and crafts and cooking or gardening. Of course, not all children will have the opportunities open to them to be able to explore such options. School clubs, the majority of which used to be run for free by the teachers in their spare time in state schools, are increasingly being replaced by paid for clubs held at the school by external providers as working parents grapple to find a solution to fill the gap between the end of the school day and when they finish work. In my opinion this is only strengthening the gap between those who can afford extracurricular activities for their children and those who cannot, creating a clear divide. The systems in place need to be made fairer and open-up opportunities for all who wish to pursue other avenues. The gains of a varied, accessible for all extracurricular activities programme, that could support working parents and allow all children to pursue their interests and socialise away from screens would far outweigh any amount of given homework and would help to create a fairer and more rounded society overall. We must remember that children will come from various home environments where parental support and access to resources maybe abundant in some and absent in others. Setting certain homework tasks comes with the risk of adding further stress and pressure to the children and their families. Instead, so many children would benefit greatly from having free access to extracurricular activities that they enjoy. It may also contribute to improved pupil well-being, which has been in steady decline in recent years, and could even help address anti-social behaviour, particularly in areas where this is a concern, by offering meaningful engagement for older students as well.

Homework Trends: Where Does the UK Fit in?

In comparison with other countries, the UK on average sets more homework than other European countries. Finland appears to be a country where students are set only a small amount of homework and yet interestingly, Finland rank consistently highly in international assessments which would suggest that homework is not a definitive factor in educational attainment overall.

In the UK, there is no national standard or requirement for teachers to set homework, nor for pupils to complete it. The amount and type of homework given can vary widely between schools, year groups and even individual teachers, often reflecting personal preferences or teaching styles. Despite this, an unspoken expectation persists – that homework is simply part of school life. But we must ask whether it is a worthwhile use of time for both teachers and pupils, and more importantly, whether the outcomes it produces are genuinely beneficial. Assigning homework purely out of tradition is not a sufficient justification.

We want pupils to develop a life-long love of learning. Learning isn't something that ceases to be once you leave school or certainly shouldn't be. It is something that continues to help you to grow as a human being throughout your life. If you have had negative learning experiences early on, you are probably less likely to want to seek further learning opportunities as you get older. We want all pupils to learn because they like learning and want to learn. We want to stir their natural curiosities and help them to discover and nurture their interests and passions. I am not convinced that set homework, particularly at primary school is conducive to this.

I'm not saying that homework should not exist at all. I think that learning could and should happen at home as well as at school, but I think we need to be really careful about what it is we are asking the children to do and consider in that their home environments, their interests, whether or not they can complete it independently or not and whether the benefits outweigh the cost of preparation by the teacher and effort and time spent by the child. In terms of inviting "flow" to find its place in the homework field, there is something to be said for leaving a "breathing space" for intrinsic motivation to fill the gap rather than filling every "nook and cranny" with extrinsic obligation created by the teacher.

Reference

National Literacy Trust. (2022). Working together towards a library in every primary school an update from the primary school library alliance. Available at: https://cdn.literacytrust.org.uk/media/documents/PSLA_report_2022__V12_SCREEN.pdf [Accessed 5 June 2025].

 The Benefits of Outdoor Learning

Learning is not something that can only happen inside a classroom and yet that is where our children spend the majority of their time when they are at school. Many early years classrooms will have access to an outdoor area where learning can more easily be taken outdoors and often is, but further up the school time outside is often limited to break times, lunch times (that's if it's not raining) and the odd P.E. lesson.

Sadly, in recent times it has been reported that schools are beginning to sell off some of their outside spaces which is, in my opinion, a tragedy. In today's world, children are spending significantly less time outdoors, due to a range of factors, from limited access to safe green spaces (as modern housing often lacks substantial garden space) to parents' work commitments that make supervised outings difficult. Added to this is the growing use of screens, with tablets and smartphones often replacing physical play. As a result, we are seeing a troubling rise in childhood obesity and mental health concerns. Now, more than ever, it is essential that schools provide safe, accessible outdoor spaces where children can play, explore and thrive.

Spending time in the outdoors, particularly in among nature is really beneficial for well-being, our physical fitness and cognitive development. Just being outdoors can help to promote fat reduction through body temperature regulation. An outdoor environment awakens our senses as you feel the breeze, hear the birds singing, smell the fresh cut grass etc. This calms our brains and together with being physically active helps the body to produce endorphins which help us to feel good and reduce the stress hormones cortisol and adrenaline. Florence Williams (author of *The Nature Fix*, 2017) has been investigating a new science of "looking at nature and our health.

The Benefits of Outdoor Learning

She describes her findings in a video available on YouTube titled "The Nature Fix – What happens when you spend just 5 minutes in nature?" and states:

> When you hear birdsong or look at fractal patterns in nature your brain puts out more alpha waves making you feel both calm and alert.
> (WWNorton, 2017)

Being both calm and alert is of course a perfect starting point to be able to absorb information and be open to learning.

Being calm and reducing stress is extremely important when it comes to children's development. If a child is stressed, maybe something is happening in their home lives, perhaps they have a phobia, maybe they've experienced trauma or any other situation that may have caused a child stress, levels of cortisol will be present in the body which can remain in the body for hours. This is a big problem because not only can it lead to developing health issues, but it also prevents a child from learning and stops their brain developing normally.

When you've been cooped up inside for long periods of time it is common to have what I can only describe as a "stuffy" feeling. A short period outside in the open air "blows away the cobwebs" so to speak, resulting in a refreshed feeling. For children, who have a natural curiosity, being outdoors (particularly amongst nature) offers an engaging environment full of natural resources where sticks and stones can become tens and ones, or the playground replaces a sheet of paper as children use chalks to practise their spellings. Inspiration can be taken from the outdoor environment for creative arts such as painting, storytelling, poetry or dance. It is also an opportunity to develop factual knowledge of flora and fauna, a breadth of knowledge that seems to be decreasing in the overall population over time. In fact, our overall connection to nature appears to have weakened over time as the population grows and we become increasingly urbanised, which is not a good thing for us nor for the environment.

Nature has been proven to benefit us in terms of both physical and emotional well-being. An article published in the Guardian (Morris, 2019) tells of a study commissioned by the National Trust which looked into the effect that hearing natural woodland sounds has on our well-being. This study focussed on three areas of well-being which included stress levels, relaxation and anxiety. It used measurements of elapsed time between listening to audio stimuli and subsequent behavioural responses. The participants in this study were divided into groups. Some listened to woodland sounds such as streams, crunching leaves and birdsong while another group listened to a voiced meditation. This study found that listening to the natural sounds had a significantly better result as it reportedly increased relaxation by up to 30% compared with no change in the level of relaxation for the group who listened to the voiced meditation or silence.

On a personal level, I find this article very interesting and relatable as it confirms the feeling that I already had that going for a walk in the woods can lift your spirits and give you a sense of feeling refreshed. I do wonder though whether it is merely the sounds alone that create this feeling of relaxation or whether it is a combination of sensory experiences, the exercise and being among the trees and foliage which are oxygen producers breathing life and renewed energy into the space that makes it so impactful on well-being. Regardless of the whys and wherefores, the evidence suggests it is good for us to be outdoors.

The Impact of Forest School

The training I received to become a Forest School leader helped inform my wider practice as a teacher and opened my eyes to see the enormous potential that learning outdoors offers. While I've always enjoyed a walk in the woods since childhood, the concept of Forest School was very new to me and different to any educational training I had, had before. What I have come to realise is how much I love this way of working and teaching children. It is more engaging and rewarding than anything I have ever tried or experienced in a classroom setting and in just a short period of time some phenomenal progress can be achieved.

During my training, I made notes on the impact that my sessions were having on three separate pupils over the course of six sessions. These notes illustrate the personal learning and progress made for each individual child. It includes the next steps for each session, showing the intentions of how to best help the children in their personal development, followed by a short reflection of the learning and progress made over the course of the six weeks. What I found most striking was how they were able to develop a range of important skills specific to their own needs and next steps that were seeing little to no development in the classroom but positively blossoming amongst the ethos and environment that Forest School provided. To protect their identities, I have named them Child A, Child B and Child C.

Child A

Child A is a Year 3 boy with high-functioning autism who struggles to cope with challenges in the classroom. He finds it particularly difficult to manage his emotions when faced with setbacks, for example, becoming distressed if he spells a word incorrectly in a test. His social and emotional skills are generally underdeveloped; he often has difficulty interpreting others' emotional cues and, at times, struggles to express his own emotions in appropriate ways.

Session 1

Child A expressed a huge interest in the mud kitchen. He spent the whole session here alongside another child, who he wouldn't normally choose to play with, and experimented with different textures of soil.

He collected water from the stream whenever he wanted to make his mixture runnier, and soon began gathering other materials to add to his creations. When he was reminded not to pick the berries, I explained our "no-pick rule" and the importance of our "respect" value, highlighting how these berries are a vital food source for birds during the winter, especially when the ground is frozen. He accepted this explanation and, showing good understanding, checked with me before collecting some fallen crab apples he had found. I told him he could use the ones on the ground and explained what they were.

This inspired him to make a "crab apple stew" and some "crab apple muffins" in the mud kitchen. It was lovely to see him use his imagination and work well alongside someone that he would not normally choose to.

Next steps:

- Aim to help to nurture this creativity and use of imagination Child A has displayed today through some storytelling and giving the mud kitchen and session a clear theme.
- Provide more opportunities for Child A to work alongside children he is less well acquainted with.

Session 2

The session started off badly for Child A today. Due to the current Covid restrictions, I am currently only allowing two children at the mud kitchen at a time. This caused problems for him as he enjoyed it so much last week that he wanted another go. Due to being told that it was someone else's turn

Teaching for Flow

today he had a bit of an emotional outburst and refused for a while to move away from the mud kitchen when the accompanying adult asked him to. I noticed that he was holding a sycamore leaf in his hand – using a distraction technique I started to ask him about the leaf. Then I suggested that if we printed it in the mud it might look like a monster footprint, just like the monster from our story at the beginning of the session. He then tried pressing it in the mud and found that although it made a print, it wasn't a very clear one. I suggested that he get a stick and draw around the leaf to make the prints stand out more. He then proceeded to make a series of "footprints" leading from the stream and up into the undergrowth. He then became completely absorbed for a while and began to tell a story. "The monster had a bath in the stream and then squelched up the path to find some food. He stomped and squelched, stomped and squelched…"

This distraction seemed to bring him back into a focussed and happy state and he later joined a group who were making a dam across the stream. Pleasingly, he also continued the storytelling theme and came back to me later on with an object (an acorn cup) he had found, to tell me a story about it. He told me that it was the monster's wart from his nose and that now it has fallen off he will grow an even bigger wart.

It was great to see the turn around in Child A from the start of the session to the end of the session. He seemed very taken with the storytelling element and this is something that I'd like to keep in these sessions as much as possible.

Next steps:

- Plan another storytelling element to next session: perhaps link with Roald Dahl.
- Plan an activity similar to the mud kitchen to ease the disappointment for children who do not get a go – perhaps George's marvellous medicine with jars and coloured water.
- Continue to help Child A to explore other avenues so he discovers more to enjoy in the forest and doesn't feel fearful if he cannot take part in a particular activity.

Session 3

The *George's Marvellous Medicine* activity went down very well with Child A today and he began with this activity. No emotional outbursts occurred due to it not being his turn in the mud kitchen and this kept him suitably engaged for the first part of the session. He enjoyed mixing the colours and

The Benefits of Outdoor Learning

enjoyed partaking in a bit of storytelling. He told me that his potion would make Granny (from the story) explode.

Towards the end of the session, he drifted off to find another group and ended up working as part of a team with some other children to carry a large log up to the fire circle so that they could use it as an extra bench. This was fantastic to see him partake in a group activity and I felt today I could see a positive step towards improved social and emotional skills.

Next steps:

- Continue to plan a focused "creative" activity to help to engage Child A from the beginning of the session and ease him in.
- Encourage and provide more opportunities for Child A to work as part of a team.

Session 4

Child A settled really well into the apple carving activity today. Despite being offered another chance to go in the mud kitchen, he turned it down and chose the apple carving activity. It was super to watch him persevere because he didn't find it particularly easy but didn't once become overwhelmed by his emotions or show frustration in the way he often would. He also took an active role in creating a display of them. He remained engaged throughout the lesson and even saw it as an opportunity to engage in some spooky storytelling with his friends whilst he was sitting around the fire circle carving his apple.

He was very keen to share a spooky story at the end of the session, but I had not allowed time for this, and he was visibly disappointed that we had run out of time. I felt I saw a big leap in Child A's emotional development today and that he was able to persevere with an activity which beforehand may have resulted in a display of frustration.

Next steps:

- Allow a storytelling time slot or even set up a storytelling area to encourage and nurture this aspect.

Session 5

In today's session, Child A worked with another child on making a 3D bonfire art piece. He was willing to go ahead and follow ideas from the other child. Child A was then immersed in role play when the other child suggested that they pretend to roast crab apples over their fire art piece. As the session progressed, they became immersed in a game, linking in the children who were working in the mud kitchen which had become the "crab apple café". At the end of the session, Child A recognised the child he had been working with for some values stickers and explained really well which values he thought they had met and why. This is a huge development for this child that he was able to spot these qualities and achievements in another person and was willing to share them.

Next steps:

- Continue to provide opportunities for Child A to work co-operatively with others in creative ways.
- Try challenging his resilience by including some problem-solving activities.

Session 6

Today Child A gravitated towards the mud kitchen again to begin with. At one point he did choose to enter the "digging" spot that I had started to layout but hadn't completed and he was digging there with a wooden spoon. He also engaged with the clay, making signs with arrows pointing the way to the mud kitchen and he also made some faces saying "look! I've made a happy face".

Next steps:

- Assign Child A the job of developing the digging area.
- Provide wooden cookies/slices and marker pens to create signs for our Forest School.

Reflections on Learning and Progress for Child A

Over the course of these six sessions, it was wonderful to see Child A's creativity and imagination flourish in the outdoor environment. He found meaningful focus through hands-on, sensory-rich activities like potion-making and apple carving, and engaged in storytelling, often building narratives from natural materials.

However, the most striking development was in his social and emotional growth. In the early sessions, he struggled to manage disappointment, but through sensitive redirection and engaging tasks, he gradually learned to self-regulate more effectively. His response to challenges noticeably improved, particularly during the apple carving activity, where he persevered with a task that he initially found difficult, without displaying frustration.

Another significant shift was in how he related to others. The moment he chose to award values stickers to his peers and explain why they deserved them marked a proud moment for me. This outward recognition of others' strengths (something he had never done in the classroom) continued in later sessions, indicating a sustained and meaningful change.

These sessions appeared to have a profound impact on Child A's emotional resilience, empathy and ability to interact positively with others. These are encouraging signs of developmental progress that would have been much harder to foster within a traditional classroom environment.

Child B

Child B is a Year 2 girl who is bright and well behaved but is reluctant to take risks and to try things that may be outside of her comfort zone. Her resilience is quite low, and she is inclined to give up on things if she finds them challenging.

Session 1

Child B struggled this session, appearing withdrawn and uncomfortable. She often stood around and watched what others were doing, not really participating herself, other than maybe to pass a stick occasionally to another child who directly asked her. She did carefully observe two different groups, watching den building by one group. At one point, with the rain making her miserable, she took herself off to the fire circle. I went over to talk to her and asked if she wanted to stand with me for a while. We talked about what we could see others doing. Eventually she was drawn to a group who had decided to build a bridge across the boggy area by the stream. She participated a bit by helping place the rocks and seemed to forget a bit about the rain. At the end of the session, she really cheered up when she realised she would get some hot chocolate and biscuits.

Next steps:

- Try to set an activity that will provide a clear focus and sense of achievement for this child, which in turn will hopefully help to build her confidence and resilience.
- Discuss clothing with her parents – is there anything additional that she can bring to make her more comfortable?

Session 2

This session was more successful and happier for child B. She spent her time in the mud kitchen alongside another member of the group, experimenting with textures and forming various ideas about what it was she was making.

> *I'm making a nice warm soup*
> *I'm making a thicker mixture, I need more mud.*
> *Let's make some cakes. We could add berries. Oh, that could be with a cherry on top.*
> *Now, I'm making melted chocolate*

It was great to see her more relaxed, content and outgoing today. She happily played along for the duration of the session and I decided to leave her to it and not intervene this session, other than to ask "what are you making?" Also, after speaking to her parents, she now has a lovely new pair of waterproof trousers that are a better fit, which no doubt contributed to an improvement in her comfort and mood today.

Next Steps:

- After seeing Child B get into her comfort zone this session, I want to offer a similar activity next session to help her to engage, for example, *George's Marvellous Medicine* activity with jars, pipettes and coloured water.
- Look for opportunities for Child B to take part in some "teamwork" activities, working as part of a bigger group with a specific role.

Session 3

Just as with Child A, this activity really helped to engage Child B from the beginning of the session. She experimented with mixing various colours, making a mental note of what colours were made when two were mixed together. She proceeded to tell others how to get the same colour saying "look, if you mix this and this it makes this colour…" I could see that she is now gaining more confidence and is feeling more comfortable in these surroundings. She remained here for the duration of the session. At the end of the session she asked if we could do some "Halloween activities" next week. It was great to see her so enthused that she was able to express a new interest.

Next steps:

- Think about a "creative activity" linked to Halloween to engage Child B from the beginning of next session.
- Find a way to help her to work more as part of a team.

Session 4

Today Child B returned to the mud kitchen cooking up a "witch's potion". She listed imaginary ingredients such as chopped worms, bat's eyes etc. she used her imagination to create various concoctions and pretend to try them out on her friends saying "oh no! You've turned into a frog".

I'm glad to see that Child B is now more confident and comfortable but I don't feel that I have moved her learning on very much at this point. She prefers to remain in her "safe zone" returning to activities she has already tried or are similar to those she has done before. I'd like to try to find ways to encourage her to explore further and develop her interests and skills.

Next Steps:

- Plan in a creative activity that requires working as part of a group that will hopefully engage child B and encourage her to try something new.

Session 5

Child B worked collaboratively with another child today to create a bonfire inspired piece of art on the woodland floor. She spent time at the beginning negotiating and deciding on the perfect spot to place their art and was fully immersed in the activity throughout the session. It was super to see her work collaboratively with another child on a different task to one she would normally opt for. She went on to suggest that they could improve their artwork and add to it by adding some "fireworks" above it.

Next steps:

- Think about other activities that will encourage Child B to collaborate with others and feel confident enough to put forward ideas.

Session 6

For the majority of this session, Child B set to work with a small group of others making puppets out of clay and a mossy stage on which to perform the puppet show. This involved teamwork, creativity and storytelling.

It was so surprising to see the difference in Child B today. When I thought back to the first session where she was withdrawn, sad and struggled to find joy in the session, today she was sad when the session came to an end. After promising that we will return next week and she could continue with the puppet activity she cheered up again. She was very proud of the fairy puppet that she made with clay. She took it away with her, planning on letting it dry and painting it ready to use in her puppet show next week.

Next steps:

- Give five- to ten-minute warning before the end of the session so she can prepare herself for the end of the session and avoid disappointment.
- Allow time next session for her to continue her activity.

Reflections on Learning and Progress for Child B

Throughout the six sessions, Child B visibly grew in terms of social skills and emotional resilience. Initially, she appeared hesitant and uncertain in the forest setting, often reluctant to engage fully in group activities. However, by the final session, there was a notable transformation in her demeanour. She not only participated eagerly but also expressed disappointment when the session concluded – a clear indicator of her increased enjoyment and comfort in this outdoor learning environment.

It was clear that the free nature and learner-led ethos of Forest School played a part in helping her to gain confidence over the course of the sessions and opened up opportunities to allow her to express herself more easily. This was particularly evident in the way she increasingly integrated into groups and began collaborating with her peers. These newly developed skills, if embedded, would be really useful tools to help her grow in all aspects of school life. Future observations could focus on how she applies this newfound confidence to other areas of learning and whether this experience has influenced her overall approach to challenges and problem-solving.

Child C

Child C is a Year 3 boy who is generally well behaved and puts noticeable effort into his learning. However, he can be easily distracted during teaching input, which often results in him missing key instructions or information. This leads to him seeking additional support to catch up or complete tasks. While not intentionally disruptive, his drifting attention suggests that sustained focus is a challenge for him in a classroom setting.

Socially, Child C gravitates towards active, physical play and particularly enjoys "rough and tumble" games with his peers, especially the other boys in the group. This energetic style of interaction appears to be a key part of how he connects with others and expresses himself in less structured environments.

Session 1

Child C displayed lots of excitement at the den building activity. Together with the other children that he chose to work with, they decided on using a mix of materials to build their den and focused mainly on building a stone surround. He worked well with the other children in the group, sometimes trying to assert his ideas, but equally listening and co-operating with others. His concentration was short though. He flitted between different activities, exploring different areas of the woodland, making a bridge across the stream and eventually returning to add more to the den. I do wonder if he just needed to explore his surroundings in this session and also whether the den building activity was too long an activity for him to gain a quick and satisfactory sense of achievement. He was also very excited to find a bird's egg to which one knowledgeable child informed him that it was probably a crow's egg. It was lovely to see the awe and wonder in his face.

Next steps:

- Think of shorter activities that match Child C's interest to prevent his concentration on the task from wavering.
- The bridge building may be a better suggested activity for next time as it will enable the child to gain a sense of achievement in a shorter period of time and he expressed an interest in this.

Session 2

Child C happily worked on his bridge/dam with a group of others today. He frequently tested it out by walking across it to determine its strength and stability and reporting back to the group whether he thought more stones were needed. I asked him about the material he had chosen as many of the other groups had used logs. He said that the stones were better because they were harder and piled on top of each other nicely. He also explained how they had chosen a narrower part of the stream so that they wouldn't need so many stones because they were quite heavy. We talked about techniques to move the stones, such as rolling.

Child C was more focussed on this one task today and tended not to flit between different activities as much but did flit between different groups mainly to test it out, add a bit to it or simply just to look at it. He co-operated well with the others in his group which was naturally formed, listening to their ideas as well as putting forward his own ideas. I had considered placing the children into groups but as it happened the groups that they formed naturally seemed to work well.

Next steps:

- Continue to allow opportunities for child C to build on these skills, learning by trial and error and collaborating with the group.
- To endeavour to find other interests to engage him in other tasks, like this one.

Session 3

Child C ignored the George's Marvellous Medicine activity and instead immediately joined a group who were making "Fantastic Mr Fox's den". Making use of the horse chestnut branches that I had to remove during my site inspection, they dragged them down to the spot where they had previously made a den with a stone surround. Child C worked with the group to help to place the branches to make a den.

He was later side tracked by someone else in the group who had found a piece of rope. Together they decided to try and find a use for the rope. They tied it around a tree and tried to make a slingshot with it. I asked Child C "Why don't you think it is working very well?" He said, "We need some elastic, so it is springy".

He then joined a group of children who were working together to carry a large log up to the fire circle.

Next steps:

- Try to engage him and teach him some more focused skills by engaging him in a slingshot activity next week.

Session 4

Unfortunately, today the catapult activity failed to engage Child C for long. It was too difficult and required too many new elements. He persevered for a while but soon lost interest due to the challenging nature of the task and drifted off to poke about in the stream.

He then found a stick with some red fungus on it and was curious to find out about it. This made me think about whether we could make use of the iPad and apps to identify things they find. This may help Child C as he has previously expressed curiosity over other natural objects he has found.

Next steps:

- Rethink the catapult activity, make it simpler to try and engage Child C
- Look into iPads and suitable Apps

Session 5

This session was much more successful in terms of creating a working catapult. I had worked out and modelled a simpler method. Child C successfully, through some trial and error, managed to get the catapult to work. He was able to remain focused on this task for a considerable amount of time before moving off to join in with the "crab apple café".

Next steps:

- Think of ways to extend an activity to try to retain interest. Perhaps we could have made a target to aim at?
- Try including a more active task with a purpose to encourage him to persevere with a task, for example, creating an obstacle course.

Session 6

It took Child C a while to settle to an activity again this session. With some gentle steering he finally settled on a well-devised game of "cricket" with a group of children. They used a stick and a crab apple and co-operated together, establishing rules and keeping score. During the game he preferred to be the bowler.

Next steps:

- Think of some more competitive game ideas that we could introduce.
- Give the obstacle course a go.

Reflections on Learning and Progress for Child C

Although the Forest School sessions have offered some benefits to Child C, particularly in developing his ability to co-operate within a group and expand his understanding of the natural world, it was difficult to determine his "muse" when it came to Forest School activities. He often flitted between activities, suggesting he was not entering a state of "flow" to optimise his learning experience.

However, it is important to remember that this was a relatively short period of time and perhaps to see a real difference in focus more time was needed. With the growing experience of more time in the woodland, I would gain more of an understanding of his interests and passions. Equally, the slow introduction of more Forest School skills and tool use which would require a greater focus, could help him to develop a greater focus and find his "flow".

Despite this, Child C has experienced several moments of achievement, whether through successfully engineering a working catapult, or working to solve simple problems when building a bridge or dam. These small but significant successes have positively impacted his confidence, motivating him to participate and engage more thoughtfully in group activities. The blossoming sense of care, interest and respect he demonstrates towards nature is heartwarming and suggests a developing sense of responsibility and stewardship for the environment.

Summary of Progress

Considering that these sessions took place over a six-week period, the progress made by each child in their personal, social and emotional development was clearly evident, albeit to varying degrees. There were also encouraging signs of cognitive growth, particularly in the children's ability to problem-solve or to identify bird eggs, fungi and other aspects of the natural environment. With thoughtful planning, the teacher could further nurture and expand this developing knowledge over time.

It was particularly interesting to observe how, despite participating in the same activities, each child engaged with the sessions in a way that was unique to their individual needs and developmental goals. Each child seemed to draw different learning experiences from the activities, demonstrating growth that was relevant and meaningful to their personal areas for development. This highlights the adaptability of the Forest School approach, where the same environment can meet diverse needs, fostering individual progress while building a sense of community.

Beyond Forest School: Other Outdoor Learning Models

Forest School is just one specific form of outdoor learning. Outdoor learning can take on other forms too such as outdoor adventure residential trips where children get to experience a range of outdoor pursuits from water sports to climbing and abseiling. However, learning outdoors does not need to be and arguably should not be limited to "specialist" activities, it should be something that is encouraged in all aspects of the curriculum. Learning outdoors helps children to apply theoretical knowledge in practical ways by enabling a more active approach to learning. For example, looking at geometrical shapes and measuring angles in an outdoor environment offers up plenty of scope for learning and can be tailored to different age groups. Inspiration for storytelling can come from outdoors from finding a locked gate and imagining what could be behind it to picking up a natural item such as a stone or stick and making up a story about it such as, "This may look like a stick but it is in fact the long-lost wand of wonders, a magical artefact belonging to the ancient woodland folk who made their homes here which in their time was a thick, dense forest…"

Deborah Lambert, Michelle Roberts and Sue Waite have authored an invaluable series of books, titled *The National Curriculum Outdoors* that provide detailed lesson plans for each curriculum subject across the primary phase, demonstrating how everyday teaching and learning can be effectively taken outdoors. These resources go beyond the more obvious outdoor lessons, such as P.E., investigating shadows in science, or reading a class book under a tree in the summer term. Instead, they reveal the extensive potential of outdoor learning across a wide range of subjects, offering creative and practical strategies to enrich students' learning experiences.

By integrating outdoor learning into the primary curriculum, these resources encourage educators to break away from the constraints of the traditional classroom and use the natural world as a dynamic, engaging and stimulating learning space. Lambert et al. (2020) effectively demonstrate that outdoor learning is not just an occasional treat but a powerful, purposeful approach to education that can be embedded across all subjects.

There are of course a number of barriers to taking learning outside. One of course being the changeable weather that we experience here in the UK. Knowing what we do already about ensuring that a child's basic needs are met to allow them to learn, this is a significant barrier if it is too cold, too hot or even too wet. To combat this, ensuring children and adults have the appropriate clothing is paramount to a successful outdoor learning approach. This can be costly and at a time when budgets are tight not just for schools but for families at home this adds an extra challenge. Inner city schools, where outdoor space maybe limited, and air quality is often compromised face greater difficulty in offering outdoor learning to their pupils. Clever designing of spaces can help to bring in more natural elements to starkly tarmacked playgrounds. Adding window boxes to grow herbs and flowers in, placing potted trees and shrubs around and even making use of rooftop spaces to create tranquil spots that attract birds and butterflies can make a difference. The more plant life that can be included the better as it can have a positive impact on air quality too.

Making use of nearby outdoor spaces such as parks or community gardens not only offers the extra space needed but also offers that chance to spend some much-needed time among nature, developing knowledge about local flora and fauna and aiding an improvement in well-being.

Better Outside: Boosting Health and Well-being

There may be staff who are reluctant to embrace the idea of outdoor learning regularly, held to the belief that behaviour is managed more easily in the confines of a classroom and being outside presents more of a challenge due to more potential for distractions, less defined physical boundaries and the added pressures of ensuring the children's safety in a less familiar and purposely "set up" environment. It is true that if your students are not used to regular outdoor activities, the initial novelty may result in an over-excitement leading to a potential disruption. However, it has been documented that regular outdoor learning can often improve behaviour and engagement in learning. According to the outdoor classroom website, outdoor learning is effective at helping to improve behaviour and minimise disruptions as it offers a "buffer zone" keeping pupils engaged in their task and offering up valuable time for the teacher to address any specific behaviour issues individually. They state:

> Outdoor learning naturally incorporates movement, providing an outlet for excess energy and restlessness. For pupils with behavioural issues, the opportunity to engage in physical activities can be a valuable outlet, contributing to improved focus and a more positive attitude towards learning.
>
> *(The Outdoor Classroom*, 2024)

For unwanted behaviours that may be triggered by a lack of sensory input, the outdoor environment offers up effortless access to a rich sensory diet which may involve swinging, tactile stimulation and proprioceptive feedback.

Spending plenty of time outdoors comes with health benefits, particularly important for children whose bodies are still growing and developing. Obvious benefits are those such as physical exercise and absorbing vitamin D from sunlight, but a lesser-known health benefit is that more time outside can have a protective effect on eyesight. Myopia (short sightedness) has become an increasing concern according to an article published in the *Journal of International Medical Research* by Zhang and Deng (2019). Interestingly, this study emphasises that increased time spent outdoors has emerged as a protective factor against the progression of myopia. The authors state:

> Among the numerous strategies implemented to slow the progression of myopia, longer time spent outdoors has come to be recognised as a protective factor against this disorder.
>
> (Zhang & Deng, 2019)

Given the stark rise in screen use in our daily lives, from tablets and smartphones to computers and television screens, the need to prioritise outdoor time has never been more critical. Prolonged screen time has been associated with eye strain and potentially worsened eyesight, making outdoor activities an important strategy in helping to protect and preserve children's vision. The above study shows that encouraging children to engage in outdoor play not only supports their physical and mental health but may also help safeguard their eyesight in a world increasingly dominated by screens.

Spending time outdoors has been shown to improve sleep, as physical activity and exposure to natural light during the day help regulate our circadian rhythms. Natural light stimulates the production of serotonin, which supports mood and alertness during the day while promoting the production of melatonin at night, helping us fall asleep more easily. Better sleep contributes to increased tolerance, perseverance and resilience which are qualities that are vital for effective learning. Well-rested individuals tend to have better focus, longer attention spans and a greater capacity to manage challenges, leading to deeper engagement in their learning experiences. By increasing the amount of time we spend outdoors in our daily lives, we can go some way to increasing our overall well-being, improve our focus and engagement and create the foundation for more productive, motivated learners.

A Summary of "Flow" in the Outdoors

Outdoor environments can help induce a state of "flow" by offering a rich, dynamic setting that encourages exploration and curiosity. The natural world provides a variety of sensory experiences and opportunities for discovery, allowing individuals to become fully absorbed in their activities and to enter that state of "flow". The types of activities that the outdoors lends itself to such as building structures, climbing or even orienteering activities keeps children interested and motivated. As mentioned earlier in this chapter, we explored the calming effects that nature and the outdoors can have on the brain, creating an ideal foundation from which a state of "flow" can emerge. The soothing influence of natural environments can reduce stress and mental clutter, allowing for deeper focus, engagement and immersion in activities.

It is without a doubt that learning outdoors comes with many significant benefits, and it is perhaps something that needs to become more ingrained into lessons throughout our primary schools. The natural world offers a wealth of scope for explorations, measured risk-taking and problem-solving – all essential skills that contribute to producing well-rounded individuals.

The case studies of the three children involved in the six-week Forest School programme provide a tangible illustration of these benefits. Each child's journey highlights the diverse and personalised growth possible, with a minimal amount of input from the teacher, whether in terms of confidence, collaboration, independence, or emotional regulation. It is arguable whether this is purely the experience of being in the outdoors or the freedom that the Forest School ethos offers. Nevertheless, it is hard to ignore the evidence that would suggest the outdoors has many benefits in terms of overall cognitive development.

Ultimately, outdoor learning is not simply an alternative approach; it is a powerful, research-backed method that can complement and enhance traditional education. With the introduction of a freer, more child-led curriculum and the combination of an increase in outdoor learning this could well turn out to be the perfect combination, or "holy grail", if you like, of a fully functioning inclusive education system.

References

Lambert, D., Roberts, M. and Waite, S. (2020). *The National Curriculum Outdoors. KS1*. Bloomsbury Education.

Morris, S. (2019, September 13). Woodland sounds help relaxation more than meditation apps - study. [online] *The Guardian*. Available at: https://www.theguardian.com/uk-news/2019/sep/13/woodland-sounds-help-relaxation-more-than-meditation-apps-study [Accessed 18 Mar. 2025].

The Outdoor Classroom. (2024). Can outdoor learning aid classroom management? [online] *The Outdoor Classroom*. Available at: https://theoutdoorclassroom.co/blog/can-outdoor-learning-aid-classroom-management [Accessed 5 June 2025].

Williams, F. (2017). *The Nature Fix: Why Nature Makes Us Happier, Healthier, and More Creative*. W.W. Norton & Company.

WWNorton. (2017, February 3). The nature fix – What happens when you spend just 5 minutes in nature? [Video] *YouTube*. Available at: https://youtu.be/iwQkTuhId-o [Accessed 18 Mar. 2025].

Zhang, J. and Deng, G. (2019). Protective effects of increased outdoor time against myopia: A review. *Journal of International Medical Research*, 48(3). Available at: https://journals.sagepub.com/doi/pdf/10.1177/0300060519893866; https://doi.org/10.1177/0300060519893866.

8 The Curriculum

The purpose of the National Curriculum is to provide a structured framework for what needs to be taught in schools, providing a consistency and equal opportunities. In recent times, the lines have become a little blurred in terms of consistency with the implementation of Free Schools and Academies who are not required to follow the National Curriculum and have the freedom to create their own. They are however, still expected to take part in national tests and it is stipulated that they must be seen to deliver a broad and balanced curriculum. As mentioned in the first chapter, the national curriculum saw its introduction in the 1980s as part of a reform of education under Margaret Thatcher's Government where it was deemed that more control measures were needed in terms of teaching and the flexibility that teachers may have had in their job roles was stripped away.

John White is a philosopher of education who has spoken extensively about the aims and values of education. In terms of primary education, he has explored its purposes and concluded that the curriculum and pedagogy should support the development of the whole child. Essentially, not just from an academic perspective but also in terms of emotional, social, moral and practical development. In an article entitled "Towards an aims-led curriculum", John White (2005) expresses his opinion that,

> Government should think harder about its proper role in curriculum-making. Since 1988 it has been obsessed with imposing a certain sort of vehicle – the traditional subject and all that comes with it.
>
> (White, 2005)

He goes on to explain how this Government-led approach is not sufficient in its inclusion nor clarity in its "aims" which he argues is where a solid curriculum plan should originate. White makes the point that teachers are best placed to generate the most effective set of intentions, providing scope for a more creative curriculum.

White's argument highlights a fundamental shift in thinking: instead of fitting pupils into pre-existing subject structures, education should begin with clear, thoughtful "aims" about the kind of people we hope pupils will become. In the primary sector, this approach would encourage educators to design learning experiences that not only build knowledge but also foster a deeper engagement, an increase in creativity and essentially more opportunities for "flow".

Following White's perspective, the role of the teacher becomes far more dynamic and creative. Rather than simply delivering content, teachers are seen as professionals who using a set of clear and meaningful aims can build on these to thoughtfully adapt their planning and teaching allowing them to meet the diverse needs and potentials of their pupils. This vision champions trust in teachers' professional judgement and values innovation in the classroom in terms of creating curriculum content.

Ultimately, with an approach such as this, there is a call for a move away from a one-size-fits-all, content-heavy model towards a more flexible, aims-led curriculum. A curriculum that places the flourishing of the whole child at its heart. The aims of an education system should drive meaningful change that reflects the needs of contemporary society, rather than perpetuating outdated ideas repackaged as innovation and rooted in old traditions and habits, as so often happens when new initiatives are introduced in education. The longer one remains in the profession, the more clearly it becomes apparent that many "'new'" ideas are simply old ones revisited. One such example of this would be the "Big Writing" initiative by Ros Wilson that then reappeared as "Writing Mastery" and along similar lines "Talk for Writing" (Pie Corbette). These all focused on structured approaches to teaching extended writing to children.

The uniformity of a national curriculum plays a crucial role in reducing disparities between regions, schools, and socio-economic groups. By providing a structured framework, it ensures that all pupils follow a clear progression of knowledge and skills that are built upon systematically and introduced at developmentally appropriate stages. This consistency helps maintain high educational standards nationwide and ensures that no student is disadvantaged due to where they live or their school's resources.

Additionally, a national curriculum safeguards against an overly narrow focus on a limited range of subjects. Without it, schools might be tempted to prioritise only core subjects, such as mathematics and literacy, at the expense of creative, practical, and humanities-based disciplines. By outlining a broad and balanced curriculum, it guarantees that pupils receive exposure to a diverse range of subjects, enriching their educational experience and equipping them with varied skills for the future.

However, while a national curriculum provides necessary structure, it must also allow for flexibility and not stifle innovation. Teachers should have greater freedom in selecting topics and tailoring lessons to meet the interests, needs, and local contexts of their pupils. Learning becomes more engaging and meaningful when educators can adapt their approach to reflect students' cultural backgrounds, community affairs such as events or issues, and general interests. A rigid, one-size-fits-all model fails to acknowledge the diversity of learners, particularly those with Special Educational Needs (SEN), who benefit from an individualised and adaptive learning pathway rather than strict age-based milestones.

Another significant challenge facing a national curriculum is the need to stay current. In an era of rapid technological advancements, evolving environmental concerns, shifting societal values, and changing political landscapes, an outdated curriculum risks leaving students ill-prepared for the modern world. A more dynamic, regularly reviewed curriculum would help ensure that young people develop relevant skills, such as digital literacy, critical thinking, and global awareness, alongside traditional academic knowledge.

While a national curriculum is essential for maintaining equity, consistency, and a broad educational experience, it must strike a careful balance. It should provide a strong foundation while allowing enough flexibility for teachers to personalise learning. It must also be adaptable, ensuring it remains aligned with the demands of an ever-changing world. A well-designed national curriculum is not just a set of standards but a living framework that evolves to meet the needs of both students and society.

The way the curriculum is currently taught is very centred around learning objectives and having in mind what you want the children to learn before the lesson begins. Supposing we flip this slightly on its head and we choose a theme, develop a range of investigatory tasks that work around that theme and make a note of the learning that has come out of it.

If we were to shift the primary national curriculum to focus on themes and investigatory tasks, rather than rigid learning objectives, it would transform the educational landscape in several significant ways. Firstly, the curriculum would consist of three core areas as outlined below:

Thematic Learning Framework

1. **Themes as Central Pillars**: The curriculum would be organised around broad, engaging themes such as "The Natural World", "Inventions", "A Step Back Through Time", or "My Community, My World". These themes would be chosen to spark curiosity and relevance in students' lives and would vary depending on year group to ensure that progression through the year groups would be consistent from school to school. For the early years' year groups there could be simpler themes, but more of them to ensure engagement such as "dinosaurs", "superheroes", "on the farm", "chocolate" etc.
2. **Interdisciplinary Approach**: Each theme would integrate subjects such as science, mathematics, language arts, history and art, encouraging students to make connections across disciplines. For instance, a theme like "The Natural World" might include science lessons on ecosystems, writing tasks including poetry or animal fact files and art projects using natural materials. This approach would ensure that a broad and balanced curriculum was available to all pupils and connections between subjects would materialise more readily.
3. **Investigatory Tasks**: Within each theme, teachers would design a variety of investigatory tasks that encourage exploration, creativity and critical thinking. These tasks could range from experiments, problem-solving tasks, school trips or even research projects. They could be linked to favourite stories that have been shared in class. For example, I once taught a lesson that was an investigation for the best material for "Cinderella's mop" with year two children. The children learned about materials and their properties and experimented and compared the absorbency of various materials. We made little Cinderella mops using clothes pegs and displayed the findings of our experiment in the classroom. The goal would be to engage students in active learning experiences that are student-centred and inquiry-based. Tools such as "TeachMate AI" could be really beneficial in the design and implementation of these tasks, again reducing the workload on teachers.

Example of a Thematic Unit

The following is a simplified example to illustrate how this approach might work in practice. We will explore additional, more detailed examples as you progress through the chapter. Naturally, in real-world settings, themes would and should be shaped by the pupils' own interests. In this case, we can imagine that the children's interest in thunder was sparked by a recent experience of a thunderstorm.

Theme: "Thunder: What's making that sound?"

- **Science**: Learning about thunder and lightning and how/why they happen. Investigating how sound travels, conducting experiments with sound waves. Learning about electricity and experimenting with circuits and different ways you can produce electricity including making a potato battery. Find out about how else electricity shows up in the natural world – electric eels for example.
- **Mathematics**: Learning about the speed of sound and light and using this to make calculations about distance. Measuring and graphing rainfall, calculating water usage and solving problems related to water distribution.
- **Language Arts**: Writing stories, newspaper articles, persuasive letters or poems about storms, reading factual books about storms, electricity and sound as well as fiction such as "After the storm" by Nick Butterworth.
- **Geography**: Learn about weather events e.g. different types of storms – snowstorms, sandstorms and why they happen. Learn about different climates around the world. Research natural disasters such as Tornados and Hurricanes – where are they located? How are they formed?
- **Art**: Research the work of William Turner and his paintings such as "Perfect Storm". Experiment with colour, form and texture to create storm inspired pictures and/or models.
- **D.T./History**– Learn about the invention of the telephone and Alexander Graham Bell. Research the history and technological advances in telephones. Investigating and experimenting with making string and cup telephones. How does it work? How do mobile phones work if they haven't got a connecting wire?

A Deeper Look at Themes as Central Pillars

While we aim to encourage learning outcomes to emerge and develop naturally, we cannot ignore the need for benchmarks to ensure consistency across the education system. However, it's equally important that we avoid forcing children into a one-size-fits-all model. This is where skilled teaching comes into its own. Teachers must draw on their professional knowledge of each child including their strengths, areas for development and where they sit in relation to age-related expectations. By doing so, they can implement the curriculum in a way that meaningfully supports progress and maximises each child's potential.

In the early years we would be looking at themes that focus on exploration, sensory learning and foundational concepts through play-based experiences. At the beginning of year one (where play is still a crucial element of learning) the themes, while still retaining some of the play-based elements, could begin to lend themselves to some structured, inquiry-based learning integrating some early literacy and numeracy connections which could look something like this:

What a Year One Themes as Central Pillars with Numeracy and Literacy Links Could Look Like

- **Our Wonderful World** – Basic geography, weather and natural habitats.
    - **Numeracy**: Measuring rainfall using simple containers, counting different types of leaves or animals and creating simple graphs such as pictograms to track weather patterns. Position and direction including compass points on a weathervane and where animals are hiding, over, under etc.
    - **Literacy**: Writing simple weather reports, reading and discussing books about nature, and creating a class story about an animal's journey through different habitats following the format of "We're Going on a bear Hunt" by Michael Rosen e.g. the camel's going on a journey. What a beautiful day. It's not scared. Uh oh! A desert. A hot, dry desert etc.

- **Stories and Structures** – Storytelling, cultural myths and moral lessons alongside the science of properties of materials (such as which materials make the strongest house).

The Curriculum

- **Numeracy**: Using fairy tale settings for problem-solving (e.g. counting the number of magic beans, simple addition and subtraction, estimating the height of Jack's beanstalk, recognising shapes in castle architecture).
- **Literacy**: Retelling and sequencing traditional stories, role playing as characters and writing alternative endings or personal versions of classic tales.

- **Wellness Warriors: Exploring Health Inside and Out** – Nutrition, exercise and mental well-being. This could include growing vegetables, learning about plants and what they need to grow and a range of mindfulness activities such as yoga, calming music and breathing techniques.
  - **Numeracy**: Sorting and classifying foods into groups, simple multiplication, counting portions of fruit and vegetables eaten in a day, and measuring heart rates before and after exercise.
  - **Literacy**: Keeping a food diary, writing recipes or instructions for making a healthy snack, and reading simple texts about the benefits of exercise and good hygiene. Write a simple list poem using adjectives and healthy foods e.g. crunchy apples, fluffy cauliflowers, sweet strawberries etc. Share the story "Eat your Greens, Goldilocks" by Steve Smallman and write a shopping list for Goldilocks with healthy foods. This could lead to writing a healthy menu, a thank you letter to the three bears and a healthy eating poster.

- **Toys Through Time** – Exploring toys from different eras and how they have changed. A brief look at different points in history. Include some design and technology and make some simple toys.
  - **Numeracy**: Sorting toys by age, creating timelines to understand historical changes and comparing toy prices from different decades using simple addition and subtraction. Data collection and simple graphs about favourite toys.
  - **Literacy**: Read the story "Dogger" by Shirley Hughes, write a diary entry for the main character "David" and write about their favourite toy. Explore how some toys work such as a clockwork toy and write simple explanation texts about how they work.

- **Seasons and Celebrations** – A look at other cultures, religions and historical celebrations including the significance of stone circles such as Stonehenge and the seasonal equinox. Understanding seasonal changes.

- **Numeracy:** Division using objects and pictorial representations e.g. sharing autumn leaves into baskets. Learning about time including days of the week, months of the year and telling the time. Understanding one more (blossom growing on trees) and one less (leaves falling in autumn). Exploring shape and sequences and looking at shapes used in certain celebrations such as stars at Christmas, hearts for Valentine's day, ovals at Easter, rangoli patterns. What shapes can you use to make a Christmas tree? Etc.
- **Literacy:** Share a range of stories from other cultures, retell and create storyboards retelling stories from other cultures. Read and write poems linked to the seasons. Design and write invitations to a celebration. Write simple information texts about different seasons or celebrations to contribute to a class book.

- **Heroes and Villains** – What makes a hero? Exploring jobs that people do and looking at some historical figures such as Florence Nightingale, Neil Armstrong, Christopher Columbus and Rosa Parks. A look at friendship and what makes a good friend, good choices and bad choices and the consequences of our choices.
  - **Numeracy**: A look at simple fractions (halves, thirds and quarters) sharing with a friend, two friends or three friends. How do we make it fair? How can you cut these shapes fairly to share with your friend? Place value – can you be a hero and locate the missing numbers? Looking at tens and ones and playing a game where if you turn over a hero you get ten points but if you turn over a villain you only get one point. How many points do I have altogether? Counting in tens and ones.
  - **Literacy**: Writing simple biographies about historical heroes. Character descriptions and simple "wanted" posters for villains. Compare a range of stories, picking out any heroes or villains and listing words to describe them. Create your own hero or villain and write about them. Speech bubbles – what might your hero or villain say?

These, of course are merely suggestions to illustrate how a whole range of age-appropriate objectives can be incorporated into a themed approach ensuring an even coverage of knowledge and skills are covered in the core subjects of numeracy and literacy. A teacher would have the autonomy to choose to spend more time on the skills and knowledge that they have assessed the children need to work on, while ensuring that all relevant objectives have been covered throughout the year. They will have the flexibility to steer the topics in the direction that children have the most enthusiasm for. Children will have more scope to reach their full potential as they are not being held back by working on a specific set group of objectives and can flourish in various directions. Schools can ensure that their curriculum is skilfully matched to their cohorts and that progression is evident in the content. It also prevents stagnation as it opens the opportunity for curriculums to be adaptable and changeable year on year.

Bringing Subjects Together: A Closer Look at Interdisciplinary Learning

Let's take year six as an example year group for this illustration of what an interdisciplinary approach may look like. The following are possible themes that could be "central pillars" in year six.

Themes would be geared towards preparing students for transition to secondary education and building their knowledge and understanding centred around global issues and leadership.

- **Community and Society** – Civic engagement, leadership and global connections.
- **Scientific Revolutions** – Major shifts in science, space exploration and medicine.
- **Ethics and Philosophy** – Debating moral dilemmas, historical movements and beliefs.
- **The Power of Media** – Journalism, propaganda and digital literacy.
- **Conflict and Resolution** – Understanding war, peace and problem-solving.
- **Futures and Possibilities** – Careers, aspirations and technological advancements.

If we take the first theme and break it down to show how we can include elements of a range of subjects within that theme making it engaging and exciting, it could look something like Table 8.1. (Remember, teachers will be driven by their knowledge of their pupils and their interests when it comes to the content, but this example illustrates how a broad and balanced curriculum can be upheld.)

Community and Society Year 6 Term: Autumn 1

Table 8.1 Shows a broken-down plan of how a broad and balanced programme of teaching can be drawn from one of the central pillar themes

Art and design	Design and technology	English
A look at street art and studying artists such as "Banksy" thinking about the messages he portrays in terms of society through his art. Explore Global Street art and compare Banksy's work with the work of artists such as Jean-Michel Basquiat. Developing skills in stencilling and building up to create a class mural.	Delve into a study of their community space and compare it with others. What are its strengths and how could it be improved? Design their own village/town/city including the things they feel are important for a thriving community e.g. green spaces, recycling centres, play areas, amenities, easy and safe access for all etc. Design and create fashion (such as a T-Shirt or Hoodie) or accessory such as a badge with a positive societal message.	Exploring persuasive language and developing skills in debating e.g. whether street art is positive or negative – looking for arguments for and against. Research an influential leader that interests them and write a biography. Share a book that features relevant themes such as "A long walk to water" by Linda Sue Park which follows the struggles of two different characters inviting comparison between different communities and societal differences. Written work can be inspired by the chosen book. Relevant grammatical teaching points can be drawn upon as part of the process. Encourage the children to learn more about a global, societal or community-based issue that sparks their want to change it. Draft and write letters to the relevant official e.g. councillors, MPs or it could even be a global company such as Lego or Amazon.

(Continued)

Table 8.1 (Continued)

Mathematics	Geography	History
Provide the scenario that if they were to be given a budget of £500, how would they put that to use to improve something in their community or school? Create a budget plan and present their work using charts. Could include percentages, addition and subtraction, data handling. Investigate and compare interesting statistics from around the world from sporting achievements to sorting and classifying strange laws.	A look at different types of communities across the world such as African tribes, Inuit people or Amish communities. What can we learn from them and their way of life? Exploring how differing climates may affect how a community operates?	Significant changes in society over time. A look at historical leaders or people who have led the way in making groundbreaking societal shifts. How law and punishment have changed over time.
Music	**Physical Education**	**Personal, Social, Health and Citizenship Education**
Exploring a range of music from other cultures and learning the distinctive sound of instruments synonymous with various places in the world such as a Sita in India, Bagpipes in Scotland or African drumming. Sound bingo matching music with the country they think it originated. Learn and sing songs from other countries. Learn about harmony.	A focus on team games and sportsmanship – supporting each other. Exploring dances from other cultures – create their own Haka dance (ceremonial dance in Māori culture) which pupils may have seen at the beginning of rugby matches.	A look at what qualities and characteristics make a good citizen and member of society. Focus on the value of responsibility. Set goals to help our communities and work towards achieving them, realising that everyone can make a small difference. This might be organising a litter pick, setting up and running a community café, running a reading club for younger children in the school at lunchtime etc.

(Continued)

Table 8.1 (Continued)

Music	Physical Education	Personal, Social, Health and Citizenship Education
Explore tempo and dynamics. Compose their own pieces using instruments, apps or online software.		
Science	**Computing**	**Modern Foreign Languages**
Discuss: *How do different countries ensure clean drinking water? What happens in places where clean water isn't available? Provide the children with dirty water (with mud, leaves, etc.) and a variety of materials (sand, cloth, coffee filters, charcoal, etc.). Children design and test their own water filtration systems experimenting with filtering, sieving and evaporation.* Compare pollution levels from different locations and discuss: *How does air pollution vary globally? How does it impact human health?* Place Vaseline-covered paper around different areas (school entrance, near roads, near trees). Leave for a few days and then examine the trapped pollutants under a magnifying glass.	Online safety and how we should conduct ourselves whilst online to protect ourselves and others. Email – converse with selected members of the community or send emails to local councillors/MPs. Play a simulation game such as "the sims" and even use programming software such as "Scratch" to create their own the sims style city creation or game. (There are useful videos on YouTube for ideas on how this can be done.)	Learn about the culture of the country of the language that has been chosen to be taught as a whole class. Who is the leader of that country? How are the communities similar to/different from ours? Learn different greetings from around the world. Use a learning programme such as Duolingo for children to either learn an additional language of their choice or to consolidate the learning taught in class.

(*Continued*)

Table 8.1 (Continued)

Science	Computing	Modern Foreign Languages
Discuss: *Which countries use the most renewable energy? How can we make energy more accessible to all communities?* Challenge pupils to design and build a simple wind turbine using cardboard, straws and a small motor. Test which blade shapes/sizes generate the most energy (linked to fair testing)		
R.E.	**Ideas for Trips**	**Events**
Discuss: *How many different religions are a part of our community?* Look at celebrations from various religions and discuss how they bring people together as a community. Faith and charity – explore faith-based charities and the role of religion in helping others.	A trip to the House of Commons/UK parliament (they offer interactive tours and workshops). Arrange a school "swap" with a school from another country. Visit a foodbank.	Plan and organise something that will benefit the community such as a community café. Select a charity and find a way to raise money for them. Invite some inspiring speakers to share their stories with the children.

There are so many directions that teachers could take to ensure that they are covering a depth of subjects and objectives while keeping it interesting, relevant and engaging for their students. Events and trips naturally provide a wealth of learning opportunities. For example, organising, setting up and running a community café can offer a wide range of valuable learning experiences across different subjects. Here are some key areas where students can develop essential skills through a real-world project such as setting up a community café:

Literacy/Computing: Looking at advertising and persuasive language, creating posters and menus using online designing software such as Canva.

Mathematics: Measure – in terms of weighing and measuring ingredients for cakes, money (budgeting, addition and subtraction) when selling the items in the café, giving change, buying ingredients, opportunities for data collection, representation (charts and/or percentages) and analysis (What was the most popular cake sold? What was the least popular? If we were to do it again, what would we do differently according to the data?)

Art and Design/Design and technology: Designing and making packaging for the items they sell.

Music/Drama: A performance could be put on for visitors to the café.

Modern Foreign Languages: Create menus or labelling in other languages (making it relevant to the community café visitors).

PSHCE: Understanding the role of volunteering and giving back to the community. Discussing and understanding what constitutes good customer service and teamwork.

With creativity and innovation, this model offers endless possibilities for providing pupils with engaging and meaningful learning experiences. Not only does it strengthen academic skills, but it also fosters essential life skills and instils the confidence to recognise that everyone has a role to play in society as a responsible and active citizen.

Inside a Progressive Investigative Learning Model

In the following section we will explore what a progressive investigatory task model based on stories may look like. (It is not necessary to base the investigations solely on stories but for the illustrative purposes of this section, I have stuck to stories to hopefully give a clearer view of what the progression may look like.) It also includes other learning opportunities that can stem from the original investigation – linking back to the interdisciplinary

The Curriculum

nature of a curriculum such as this. I have included two examples for each year group based on popular stories.

Reception/Foundation Stage

Story: The Three Little Pigs
   Investigation: *Which material makes the strongest house?*
   Children explore different building materials by constructing small houses using straw, sticks and building blocks in the outdoor area. They test their strength using a fan to simulate the wolf's breath.
   Expanding the Learning and Following Children's Interests:
   This investigation can spark curiosity about real buildings and historical events. For example, links can be made to the Great Fire of London:

- What were buildings made of in the past?
- Why and how did the fire spread so quickly?
- How do modern buildings keep us safe?

To extend learning further, children could:

- Meet real firefighters in a school visit to learn about fire safety.
- Transform the role play area into a fire station, with helmets, hoses and radios for imaginative play.
- Conduct a hands-on experiment testing which materials burn more easily, using safe, controlled demonstrations (e.g., watching a candle and discussing fire safety).
- Music – Sing London's burning and learn about singing in a round, playing percussion instruments and using musical notation to learn to play the tune using xylophones or a piano app on iPads.

By following the children's interests, this theme can evolve into deeper explorations of materials, safety and historical events, making learning even more meaningful.

Story: Peter Pan
   Investigation: Exploring Shadows with Peter Pan
   The children could explore shadows outside, learning about the sun and its position throughout the day – what happens to our shadows at different

Teaching for Flow

times of day. They could use torches to explore shadows – experimenting with different objects and distances.

Expanding the learning and following children's interests:

The children could go on to make shadow puppet theatres, retelling stories they know and creating their own. This could lead to some opportunities for writing.

- Who are your characters?
- Where is your story set?
- What will happen at the beginning, in the middle and at the end of your story?

To extend learning further, children could:

- Explore light and how it splits into rainbow colours using prisms.
- Experiment with colour mixing and learn the colours of the rainbow.
- Explore colour changes and create a magic rainbow with coffee filter paper.

The direction in which the sessions progress will depend upon the interests of the group and your observations as a teacher to assess what skills need developing and where you notice a state of "flow" occurring.

Year One

Story: The Gruffalo by Julia Donaldson

Investigation: Which food do the animals in the story like best?

In the story, the Gruffalo is described as liking different foods (roasted fox, scrambled snake, owl ice cream). This investigation explores what real animals like to eat!

Set up a food testing station where children predict and test which foods different animals (or birds) prefer. Place small amounts of different foods (seeds, fruit, bread, cheese) outside and observe which ones local birds or insects are most attracted to – a video camera could be set up to monitor the feeding stations for night-time observations. Children could experiment by making different bird feeders, thinking about different designs and materials.

The Curriculum

Expanding the Learning and Following Children's Interests:

- Learn about carnivores, herbivores and omnivores – what do real owls, foxes and snakes actually eat?
- Learning about simple food chains.
- Nocturnal animals versus daytime animals – could use the book "Wow said the Owl" by Tim Hopgood to help create discussion.

Ideas to extend learning further could include:

- Writing fun list poems about different foods, or even recipes. The book "Beware of Boys" by Tony Blundell is a great one for learning how to write recipes in a fun way.
- Talk about our favourite foods and look at food from other cultures.
- Create simple charts to display favourite foods – this could be made more hands-on by using multilink cubes to build a bar chart, making it both practical and interactive.
- Cooking.

Story: "Max" by Bob Graham
Investigation: Which Material would make the best Superhero Cape?
Discuss what qualities a superhero cape would need and why. This could lead to children experimenting with a variety of materials (paper, cardboard, fabric, foil) by pulling, stretching or adding weight.
Expanding the learning and following children's interests

- Explore how superheroes fly and explore forces such as air resistance and gravity.
- Design and make a superhero cape – a role play area could be set up where children create, test and improve their designs.
- Make and test parachutes to see how we can slow down a falling action figure.

Ideas to extend learning further could include:

- PSHCE lesson about celebrating differences using Max as a talking point – How was he different? What could our superpowers be? e.g. helping others

Teaching for Flow

- Explore the topic of flight including aircraft and birds – experiment with paper aeroplanes and set up a bird hide to watch birds.
- Include some maths by keeping a tally of birds and measuring the distance a paper aeroplane travels.
- Create your own superhero and write a story about them – what would their name be? What superpower would they have? What problem would they solve?

Year Two

Story: "The Pirates Next Door" by Jonny Duddle
Investigation: How do Pirates stop their ships from floating away? An investigation into the best anchor – which shape holds the strongest? The children could test different anchor shapes (e.g., a stick, a curved hook, a heavy rock) in a tray of sand or water to see which grips the best. They could discuss how real anchors work and why their shape is important.
Expanding the learning and following the children's interests:

- Explore other parts of a ship (rudder, propeller and sail) and find out how they work. This could lead to drawing diagrams and writing explanatory texts.
- Build mini pulley systems to test how heavy objects can be lifted (like pulling up an anchor).
- Design and make model boats/ships.

Ideas to extend learning further could include:

- Learning about oceans and seas around the world.
- Creating and reading maps to find treasure.
- Reading co-ordinates.
- Learning about historical ships and events such as the Titanic.

Story: "How to catch a dragon" by Carly Hart and Ed Eaves
Investigation: How can we make a moving dragon?
For this investigation the children will learn about pneumatic systems using two syringes and a piece of plastic tubing. They could be set the challenge of experimenting to see if they could design and make a dragon or

monster that can open and close its mouth. They could do this by attaching one syringe to a dragon or monster's mouth (made from card or paper) and when they push a second syringe (joined by a piece of plastic tubing to the first one), air moves through the tube pushing the other syringe out and making the dragon or monsters mouth open.

Expanding learning and following the children's interests:

- Can they experiment to make different parts move? (e.g. wings, arms). Engineering challenge – can they make a model with multiple moving parts?
- Learn about how pneumatic systems are used in real life such as air brakes on buses, fairground rides and even robots.
- Make a stop-go animation using their model dragon and a knight made from plasticine.
- Exploring capacity and volume – investigating how much air different syringes may hold.
- Measuring angles – use a protractor to measure the angle of the mouth when fully open. Is it an acute or obtuse angle?

Ideas to extend learning further could include

- Work centred around the story of George and the Dragon – writing, drama and puppet theatre performances.
- Learn about castles and knights.
- Learn about dragons in other cultures such as China and learn about Chinese New Year.

Year Three

Story: "The Iron Man" by Ted Hughes

Investigation: The Iron Man's Magnetic Mission – How could we help the Iron Man find lost metal objects?

This investigation involves classifying a range of objects into magnetic and non-magnetic groups. Once they have gained an understanding of what a magnetic material is, they could use this to create a maze using card and place a magnetic object such as a paperclip representing the character of the Iron Man inside. Using a magnet underneath they must guide the character (magnetic object) out of the maze.

Expanding learning and following the children's interests:

- Discovering how magnets are used in everyday life such as in a compass, cupboard doors and even inside electronics such as computers and smartphones.
- Make a magnetic fishing game.
- Explore magnets repelling each other to make things levitate like magic!

Ideas to extend learning further could include:

- Learning about the Earth and its magnetic field leads to learning about other planets and the solar system.
- Compass points and have a go at making a compass by rubbing a needle or small nail against a magnet about 50 times in the same direction followed by carefully floating it on a small piece of cork in water – watch it align with north!
- The story features farms and so this lends itself nicely to explore life on a farm and a look at farm machinery.
- Work on similes, powerful verbs and adjectives using the story for inspiration.

Story: "The Worst Witch" by Jill Murphy
Investigation: The Worst Witch's Potion Mixing

The idea behind this investigation would be to test the solubility of different ingredients (such as sugar, salt, flour and coffee) in water. Discuss what dissolves best? Experiment with different temperatures of water, measuring the temperature with a thermometer.

Expanding learning and following the children's interests:

- Investigate if the process is reversible. After dissolving different substances in water, test ways to separate them again through filtering and learning about evaporation and condensation.
- Deeper learning about solids, liquids and gases.
- Can we make a magic potion that changes colour? Introduce acids and bases in a simple way. Experiment using red cabbage water as a pH indicator. Add:
    - Lemon juice (acid) → Turns pink
    - Baking soda (alkali) → Turns blue/green

The Curriculum

Further Challenge:
- o   Can they turn it back to its original colour?
- o   What happens if they mix both an acid and an alkali together?

Ideas to extend learning further could include:

- Experiment with maths magic tricks such as a "Mind-Reading" Number Trick involving addition and place value. Tell a child to pick a number between 1 and 10. Ask them to:

1. Double the number.
2. Add 8.
3. Divide by 2.
4. Subtract the original number.

The answer is always 4!

The learning included here is understanding how numbers change when they are doubled, halved, added to, and subtracted from. It also encourages logical thinking and pattern recognition.

Or they could try a "card trick" involving logic sequences. The teacher takes 21 playing cards and lays them in 3 columns of 7 cards. Ask the child to pick a card (but don't tell you which one!). They only tell you which column it's in. Gather the cards, keeping that column in the middle and repeat the process twice. After the third time, the chosen card will be the 11th card in the pile!

This idea helps children follow sequences and patterns and encourages logical thinking and reasoning.

- Exploring friendships and overcoming challenges (personal, social, health and citizenship education) just as the main character "Mildred" in the "Worst Witch" stories finds herself having to do. What makes a good friend? What steps can we take to overcome our own challenges?
- The children could design and take part in their own broomstick obstacle course. This could lead to exploring other magical themed sports such as Quidditch from Harry Potter and they could design their own game and write a set of instructions on how to play.

Teaching for Flow

Year Four

Story: "Vacation under the volcano" by Mary Pope Osborne

Investigation: Eruption Exploration: Which Mixture Makes the Biggest Volcano Eruption?

For this investigation, children could test different ratios of baking soda and vinegar (or lemon juice) to find the most dramatic reaction. They could predict and record results with changes in the amount of each ingredient and make a working model of a volcano.

Expanding learning and following children's interests:

- Think about how we use chemical reactions in real-life situations such as in an instant cool pack.
- Fermentation such as in yeast and bread making.
- Chemical reactions within our bodies for example in digestion.

Ideas to extend learning further could include:

- Learning about ancient Romans and Pompei.
- Recognise, read and write Roman numerals including on a clock face.
- Learn about time and look at sundials.
- Study and create mosaics.
- Research and find out about other natural disasters and what causes them such as earthquakes and tornados.
- In keeping with the time period, making the use of papyrus paper and a reed pen – the children could investigate using natural resources to make paper and writing implements.

Story: "When Charlie McButton Lost Power" by Suzanne Collins

Investigation: How could we help Charlie McButton with his electrical problem? Making a potato battery.

For this investigation children will need to have some understanding about circuits and can experiment with making working circuits. They can then have a go at making a potato battery which works by causing a chemical reaction between a potato, copper and zinc to produce electricity. To make one you can cut a potato in half, insert a galvanised nail into one end of the potato and a penny into the other end.

The Curriculum

Expanding learning and following children's interests:

- Learn about conductors and insulators and investigate which materials are good conductors of electricity. Build a simple circuit and test materials (metal, wood, plastic, rubber) to see which conduct electricity.
- Experiment with switches and design and make their own torch.
- Learn about other sources of electricity and explore renewable energy forms such as hydroelectricity, wind power and solar power.

Ideas to extend learning further could include:

- Learning about and experimenting with static electricity.
- Finding out about electricity in nature such as electric eels and lightning strikes.
- The class could have a debate about whether they think the use of electricity has a positive or negative effect on us.
- Delve deeper into environmental issues and write a persuasive letter to the local MP expressing their thoughts and feelings on environmental factors that are important to them.
- Learn about influential people when it comes to the environment such as David Attenborough and Greta Thunberg.

Year Five

Story: "The Waterhorse" by Dick King Smith

Investigation: Water resistance and streamlining – How can the water horse swim faster?

Discuss the body shape and movements of the water horse that help it to move efficiently through the water. Children investigate how differently shaped boats move through the water by creating model boats and testing them. They could explore the effect of streamlining compared to bulky shapes – which moves the fastest when powered by a fan? They could also experiment by adding fins or ridges.

Expanding learning and following the children's interests:

- Learn about Donald Campbell and "The Bluebird K7" which was a jet-powered hydroplane. The hydroplane was revolutionary for its time and was designed to beat the water speed record.

- Research other aquatic animals, thinking about their body shape and how they move through the water.
- Experiment with viscosity to see if or how it affects water resistance. For example, shape some plasticine into a streamlined form and drop the shape into various liquids (water, cooking oil, saline solution, honey) timing how long it takes to sink. Compare the times to see how the viscosity affects water resistance.

Ideas to extend learning further could include:

- Finding out about Scotland, the Lake District and/or mountain ranges such as the Alps in terms of geography, customs and traditions.
- Discovering more about mountains, lochs and lakes.
- Debating whether they believe the Lochness monster to be real and creating persuasive arguments for or against.
- Learning more about boats, ships and yachts and researching boats from history such as The Mary Rose.

Story: The Wild Robot by Peter Brown

Investigation: Camouflage – Can we design and build a mini shelter to camouflage Roz?

In the book, Roz the Wild Robot spends time with the animals in the wild. Imagining she must learn to camouflage herself to protect herself from predators, provide children with different natural materials (leaves, sticks, mud, moss, bark, straw, hay, etc.). Outside, children design and make mini shelters testing which materials blend in best with the background by photographing them from different angles.

Extending learning and following the children's interests:

- Compare light vs dark materials – which blends best with different environments.
- Think about how the time of year may make a difference to how well our camouflage may work – what might we need to change in the summer compared to the winter?
- Think about animal camouflage and adaptations – how do chameleons, snow hares and tigers blend in?
- Find out about military and survival technology – how do humans use camouflage?

Ideas to extend learning further could include:

- Discovering other survival skills including simple campfire cooking, first aid and navigation skills.
- Study Bear Grylls and write a biography.
- Investigate how animals adapt to eat different foods. In the book, Roz learns to survive by watching the animals. Provide children with different tools (tweezers, chopsticks, spoons, pipettes) and ask them to test which tool is best for picking up different "foods" (rice, seeds, marbles, string, water).
- Explore how animals have adapted to extreme environments.
- Learn about Darwin's finches and evolution.

Year Six

Story: Sherlock Holmes by Arthur Conan Doyle (There are various books available as a children's collection)

Investigation: Can you solve the mystery of the missing manuscript?

Create a "breaking news" style announcement that a valuable manuscript containing a lost Sherlock Holmes story has been stolen from a local museum. Describe the museum, manuscript and circumstances of the theft to set the scene. Introduce the idea that they are going to be detectives, working to solve the mystery, just like Sherlock Holmes. Provide the children with some sample suspect interviews containing clues and red herrings that students must analyse, looking for inconsistencies and potential motives. They must collect and analyse evidence such as studying fingerprints, a torn piece of paper with a partial message, a coded message and a dropped item (e.g. a ticket stub, a button), riddles, anagrams, simple ciphers and even maps. This could lead to children producing their own case report and a presentation of their findings.

Extending learning and following the children's interests:

- Explore and learn about various forms of coding and logic puzzles.
- Design their own puzzles and coded messages for a friend to solve.
- Explore how fingerprints are unique by using ink pads and magnifying glasses.
- Make links to the codebreakers in the Second World War who worked at Bletchley Park.

Teaching for Flow

Ideas to extend learning further could include:

- Learning and using Morse Code to send messages to each other.
- Research and write a biography about Arthur Conan Doyle.
- Exploring the Victorian and Edwardian eras, which are when the Sherlock Holmes stories are set.
- An investigation of crime and punishment through time including a look at how advances in technology have helped to solve crimes.
- A visit from a police detective to talk about their job in a real-life context.
- Study the features that make a good detective story and use this knowledge to write your own effective detective story.

Story: Harry Potter and the Philosopher's Stone by J. K. Rowling
Investigation: How do crystals form?

In this experiment children experiment with growing crystals using a simple salt and sugar solution. Using warm water, children gradually add salt or sugar stirring constantly until no more will dissolve. Add some food colouring if you want coloured crystals. Tie a piece of string to a lollypop stick and lay the stick across the top of the container holding the solution allowing the string to hang down into it without touching the sides or bottom of the container. Leave it undisturbed for about a week, but during this process observe the crystals forming, noting any changes taking place.

Extending learning and following the children's interests:

- Create some crystal art letting pupils create shapes with pipe cleaners, growing crystals on these to make different crystal sculptures or their own "Philosopher's stone".
- Investigate using different substances (e.g. salt, sugar, baking soda) to create the solution to compare how the crystals form.
- Create a graph to show the data they collected as they observed their crystals growing over time.
- An exploration of atoms and molecules

Ideas to extend learning further could include:

- A look at geology learning about rocks, minerals and landforms and exploring the composition, structure and formation of rocks. This could also include exploring what fossils are and how they are formed.

- Thinking about how weather affects the formation of rocks and crystals.
- Looking at natural rock formations or famous landmarks around the world such as Durdle Door, Wave Rock, The Grand Canyon, The Giant's Causeway.
- The book touches on themes of courage and resilience as the main character faces numerous challenges and finds himself navigating his way through adversity which offers up the opportunity to explore moral dilemmas, social differences and how the children could show courage and resilience in different given scenarios.

You may notice that as you progress through each year group the texts and investigations become more challenging and aim to build upon previously gained knowledge and experience, deepening understanding. The expectations grow in the complexity of knowledge they are expected to gain and what they produce as an outcome of their learning. These are of course only a small sample of what could be achieved yet the potential to achieve a variety of knowledge, skills and age-appropriate objectives within a number of different subjects is clear.

Statutory and Routine Curriculum Essentials

To help children develop essential skills and strong foundations, enabling them to fully engage in the rich, exciting learning opportunities around them, it's crucial to embed daily opportunities for playful, meaningful practice into their routine. For younger children, rather than rigid, teacher-led sessions, children should be encouraged to explore subjects, including literacy and numeracy, in ways that feel natural and engaging to them.

Phonics and Reading Skills: Phonics, e.g. can be woven into storytelling, games and real-world interactions, rather than being limited to a fixed 15–20 minute lesson. Similarly, number fluency can develop through hands-on activities like puzzles, movement-based counting games and real-life applications such as measuring, budgeting or pattern-spotting. One-on-one reading with an adult (at least twice a week, but more often for those who need it) should be a collaborative, enjoyable experience where children are empowered to choose books that excite them, fostering a genuine love of reading.

Spelling Focus Input: For older children, spelling should be reinforced through engaging, interactive activities rather than rote memorisation. A variety of spelling games can be used, with specific spelling rules taught in fun and memorable ways, such as rhymes (most of us recall "I before E except after C"), mnemonics and raps. The teacher's assessment of students' needs should guide these activities, ensuring targeted support that effectively aids progression.

Key Maths Skills: Similarly, key maths skills, such as multiplication tables, can be strengthened through daily bursts of shared songs, helping students gain familiarity with them in an enjoyable way. However, there is one particular maths skill that often doesn't receive the attention it truly requires, and that's telling the time.

If you've ever been a primary school teacher, you'll understand the struggle of teaching time. It's one of the hardest concepts to master, requiring consistent exposure and vast amounts of practice before it "clicks" with students. Traditional, one-off lessons or even a focussed week are rarely effective on their own. Instead, telling the time should become a daily, purposeful task, seamlessly woven into the routine.

By actively involving children in time management, they will regularly read the time, calculate how long they have left for tasks and naturally think about time increments. This not only strengthens their ability to tell the time but also fosters self-awareness and personal time management skills, a crucial life skill often dictated solely by the teacher. When children learn to track their own time, they begin to self-regulate, make adjustments and develop a greater sense of responsibility for their learning and productivity.

A Balance of Routine and Freedom: Establishing a familiar yet flexible routine helps children feel safe while giving them autonomy in their learning. To maintain motivation, structured play-based activities, storytelling and music can be powerful tools. For example, children can reinforce multiplication facts by adapting popular songs, such as the "6 Times Table Song", set to the tune of Taylor Swift's *Shake It Off*. (Examples such as this can be found on YouTube.) Encouraging children to create their own songs, dances or stories around key concepts allows them to actively construct knowledge, rather than passively receive it.

By prioritising joy, autonomy and connection, we ensure that children aren't just memorising facts, but they are building the confidence and curiosity to explore and extend their learning in ways that are meaningful to them.

When building a curriculum, it will be important for schools to ensure fair and even coverage of a range of age-appropriate topics within a broad collection of subjects, but these subjects do not need to exist as stand-alone. By creatively linking subjects, discovering and leaning into the children's interests and finding engaging ways to deliver the knowledge and skills that the children need to develop (established by the observations and assessments of the teacher) we can achieve a learning system that opens up more opportunity for "flow" to occur.

Curriculum Flexibility and Adaptability

Adaptable Learning Paths: The curriculum would allow for flexibility to accommodate students' interests, needs and learning paces. Teachers would have the autonomy to adapt themes and tasks based on the dynamics of their classrooms, ensuring that learning remains relevant and engaging for all students.

Collaboration and Group Work: Emphasis would be placed on collaborative learning experiences. Group projects and peer learning would be encouraged, fostering teamwork, communication skills and a sense of community within the classroom. (This is something that seems all the more significant after cohorts of children missed out on such opportunities for periods of time during the COVID pandemic.)

Assessment and Documentation

It would seem of course that a curriculum comes hand-in-hand with assessment and recording systems in order to keep a log of the learning that has taken place. We will take a closer look at assessment and the changes that are needed and why in a later chapter, but here are some necessary changes, complementary to the way in which a thematic-based curriculum would work that need to be considered when creating and implementing a curriculum such as this.

1. **Learning Portfolios**: Instead of traditional tests and grades, teachers and students would compile learning portfolios documenting their projects, discoveries and "Wow, I did it!" moments. It may also be helpful to

record their reflections (particularly with older children) with the aim to encourage greater ownership over their personal learning journey. These portfolios would serve as a comprehensive record of their learning journey, showcasing their progress and achievements over time.
2. **Reflective Practices**: Regular reflection sessions would be incorporated, where students discuss what they have learned, challenges they faced and how they overcame them. This reflective practice would help students develop metacognitive skills and a deeper understanding of their own learning processes. It would also help students to develop a growth mindset which is vital for lifelong learning and self-esteem.
3. **Teacher Observations and Anecdotal Records**: Teachers would play a crucial role in observing and documenting students' learning experiences. Anecdotal records and observational notes would be used to track students' progress and provide personalised feedback, ensuring that each child's learning needs are being met. It will no longer be necessary to mark children's books or stamp them with "Verbal Feedback" stamps because a more meaningful process will have taken place through discussion and reflection during the learning process. Crucially, this would reduce workload and create more time for teachers to focus on the creation and input which will really make the difference to the learning that takes place.

Professional Development and Support

Teacher Training and Support: To successfully implement this approach, teachers would receive ongoing professional development focused on inquiry-based learning, project management and reflective practices. Support networks, such as school partnerships and collaborative planning time would be essential to help teachers share ideas and strategies. Use should be made of new technologies such as "TeachMate AI" which would be an ideal tool to assist teachers with many of these tasks.

Resource-Rich Environments: Classrooms and schools would be equipped with diverse resources, such as technology, manipulatives and access to nature, to support varied investigatory tasks. Community partnerships with local organisations, museums and experts would further enrich the learning experience.

By adopting this thematic and investigatory approach, the primary national curriculum would avoid becoming stagnant and would allow teachers to do what they do best – teach with enthusiasm, expression and creativity. Not only will it foster deeper engagement and motivation among students but also cultivate a love for learning, critical thinking and creativity. This shift would better prepare students for the complexities of the modern world, equipping them with the skills and mindsets needed to thrive in diverse and ever-changing environments.

Reference

White, J. (2005). *Towards an aims-led curriculum*. Qualifications and Curriculum Authority. [online] Available at https://dera.ioe.ac.uk/id/eprint/9704/1/11482_john_white_towards_an_aims_led_curr.pdf [Accessed 5 June 2025].

Continuous Provision

Continuous provision refers to a thoughtfully designed classroom setup that fosters structured play, allowing children to learn and develop skills independently. This approach is primarily associated with the Early Years curriculum, though some schools extend it into key stage one. However, it is rarely seen by the time children reach key stage two. Continuous provision prioritises child-centred, self-directed learning over a strict timetable of activities, creating an environment conducive to achieving a state of "flow". While there seems to be no statistical evidence directly comparing continuous provision with a structured timetabled approach, many educators are increasingly favouring this method. Although it takes careful planning and thought about the classroom layout and resources available, it is a much less restrictive teaching method which opens up a multitude of possibilities. McHugh in an article entitled "What is continuous provision?" explains how well-planned and executed continuous provision supports children to "learn skills", "challenge their thinking" and "embed concepts". McHugh goes on to say:

> It should also provide the context for a variety of learning conversations between children and adults with rich opportunities for modelling and extending speech and vocabulary. It is within this learning environment that the children will also develop key learning attributes.
> (McHugh, 2024)

Why Only the Younger Year Groups?

Why does continuous provision often disappear as children progress through school? From my experience working in primary schools, one of the main factors is the overwhelming focus on SATs. The current education system emphasises a repetitive cycle of planning, teaching and assessing to ensure children retain and apply the specific knowledge required to pass these tests. While this may seem a stark perspective, it is a realistic one.

Many educators view continuous provision outside of the early years as a hindrance to covering the rigid, test-focused curriculum, which demands children demonstrate specific skills, such as identifying expanded noun phrases or fronted adverbials. Ironically, these grammatical exercises rarely improve writing quality. Following the introduction of the grammar tests by Michael Gove in the early 2010s, I noticed that children's writing often lost its creativity. Both teachers and students became so preoccupied with including mandated grammatical features that the joy and artistry of composition began to suffer.

One of the pleasures of writing is experimenting with language to set a tone or create an effect, which can involve bending grammatical rules. Writers such as Irvine Welsh in *Trainspotting* capture dialects through unconventional grammar, while Roald Dahl's *The BFG* delights readers with playful, invented words. James Joyce's *Finnegan's Wake* employs deliberate grammatical errors which some believe to portray memories or a dreamlike state. These creative liberties demonstrate that great writing isn't bound by rigid rules.

Michael Rosen, the well-known and much-loved Children's author (who famously wrote *We're Going on a Bear Hunt*) has been vocal about the impact of the curriculum and grammar teaching in primary schools. In his analysis of the key stage two grammar, punctuation and spelling test, he highlights its inaccuracy and the confusion it causes children, who are taught rules that the literature they read can, at times, contradict. Rosen argues that these tests are less about improving literacy and more about measuring teacher performance. His detailed critique can be found on his blog: "Michael Rosen: This year's KS2 Grammar, punctuation and spelling test – analysed" (Rosen, 2024).

It is abundantly clear from his analysis that he believes the tests are not only highly flawed but also confusing and discouraging for children. Children are taught specific rules that are sometimes contradicted by the books they read but which they are told they must employ to be a "good writer". Furthermore, he argues that the tests were primarily designed as another tool to evaluate teacher performance rather than to enhance students' understanding or love of language.

It is somehow seen, as children get older, to be holding them back if they are allowed to spend too much time engaging in play. Although there is plenty of evidence out there that would suggest (from a learning, developing and neuroscience perspective) that play is really beneficial when it comes to contextual learning and building neural pathways. Good continuous provision invites and facilitates learning through more of a play-based approach compared to a more formal style typically seen across key stage two classrooms. It requires a teacher to take on a more passive role as facilitator rather than as an active knowledge disseminator. It shifts the focus more to the learning process leaving it open to varied and, by the nature of it, differentiated outcomes as opposed to more of a content focus with one specific intended outcome.

A brief case study by Aiden Severs entitled "Continuous Provision and EYFS-Inspired Practice in key stage 2" gives an example of how a school incorporated continuous provision throughout the year groups, including key stage two. The school found that there were several positive outcomes in terms of the children's learning and development that came as a result of this method, including better engagement, greater autonomy and core subjects such as Maths and English did not appear to be hampered (as some may fear). The one point that stood out the most to me was that his assessment of the children, through verbal means found,

> ...they are knowledgeable and can remember prior learning from other units of work. In fact, children have learned things beyond the scope of the key knowledge specified in the curriculum – this as a result of that more self-directed time and those gateway key facts.
>
> (Severs, 2024)

This successful implementation of continuous provision in key stage two highlights its potential to create an environment conducive to "flow". By allowing children more autonomy and opportunities for self-directed learning, the approach fosters deeper engagement and sustained focus, all of which are key components of achieving a "flow" state. The case study demonstrates how this can lead to enriched learning experiences, with children not only meeting but often exceeding curriculum expectations. This aligns with the principles of "flow", where intrinsic motivation and meaningful engagement enable learners to absorb and retain information more effectively. The case study school's implementation of continuous provision in key stage two proves that structured play and self-directed exploration can be successfully implemented further up the school, paving the way for a more holistic approach to education.

The current education system, heavily driven by the national curriculum and statutory tests, often prioritises ensuring children are taught everything deemed necessary within its framework. Curriculum coverage carries significant weight, providing a shared agenda for schools to follow. It's understandable that any approach challenging this structure might generate controversy and resistance. Schools are highly target-driven and accustomed to meeting specific objectives, so a less structured, more open-ended concept might feel unfamiliar, less controlled and even unsettling.

However, if we reflect on the findings of the case study mentioned earlier and consider the broader possibilities, it becomes evident that the current approach (where continuous provision is not widely used beyond the early years) may inadvertently limit children's capacity to learn. By focusing strictly on national curriculum content and teaching to the tests, we risk narrowing the scope of their education and stifling opportunities for deeper exploration and discovery. Continuous provision, in contrast, removes these limitations, fostering a more open-ended and dynamic learning environment. This approach has the potential to expand children's development and understanding, unlocking greater opportunities for them to absorb and apply new information.

An important point to note here too is that educating teachers on what continuous provision actually is, is vital to ensure understanding and make the move towards this form of practice easier. It does not mean that there is no longer any teaching input and that children are just allowed to go off and choose whatever they want to do. As the scholastic website points out it is merely an extension of the taught curriculum but at the same time fosters independence.

> Think of continuous provision as an approach to continuing the taught aspects of a curriculum through independent enquiry. It is the provision of open-ended resources and challenges, offering a multitude of routes to learning, where the children decide what they want to do.
>
> (Luton, 2018)

The Challenges of Incorporating Continuous Provision

Perhaps the biggest challenge that we face is the change in the way in which we plan, resource and set up our classrooms to enable effective continuous provision to take place. Classrooms need clearly defined zones for different types of learning, such as creative, sensory and exploratory activities, which can be time-consuming and resource-intensive to set up.

Furthermore, planning for continuous provision involves anticipating how children might engage with the space and designing activities that balance freedom with purposeful learning opportunities. This demands a shift in mindset, from delivering fixed lessons to creating environments that allow for autonomy while subtly guiding children towards key objectives. These are all new skills that require time to develop and become fully embedded throughout the primary phase.

Another drawback that may be found to incorporating continuous provision further up the school is the issue of space. Space is required to enable an effective continuous provision set up. It requires classrooms to have a completely different set up with resources available throughout the day and defined learning spaces rather than one open space filled with tables and chairs. This could be seen as a significant drawback for many teachers, given the time and effort required to design an effective classroom layout within the constraints of the space available. This challenge is particularly evident in key stage two, where class sizes are often larger than in the earlier years. Unlike key stage one where there is a limit cap of 30 pupils per class, there is currently no cap on class sizes in key stage two.

One potential solution to this issue is to incorporate outdoor learning by using outdoor spaces as an extension of the classroom. During my Forest School training, I gained a deep understanding of the many benefits an outdoor learning environment offers. As we looked at in Chapter 7 "the benefits of outdoor learning", there is research which shows that spending time outdoors, especially in nature, helps lower stress levels, which enhances the brain's ability to absorb and process information. Being outside engages all our senses (sounds, smells, textures and even the way we perceive temperature) helping to ground us and improve focus.

Outdoor learning also encourages physical activity, which is particularly important in today's technology-driven world, where gaming devices, smartphones and tablets often promote sedentary habits. Physical activity is not only beneficial for physical health but also for mental well-being. It triggers the release of feel-good hormones, helping us reset, refresh and refocus.

Schools have long recognised the link between activity and concentration, incorporating short bursts of movement into the school day to re-energise pupils. Strategies such as movement breaks, energetic exercises, or meditation sessions are often used to help children regain focus after breaks, tests, or extended periods of concentration. However, a continuous provision approach could potentially reduce the need for these structured breaks. By naturally integrating activity and engagement into the learning process, continuous provision keeps children actively involved and more attentive throughout the day.

Although existing evidence supports continuous provision as an effective approach to teaching and learning, there is arguably insufficient research specific to its implementation in key stage two to provide substantial weight to its effectiveness at this level. This is largely because it remains an uncommon practice. Schools often appear constrained by the pressure to demonstrate that their pupils are making the expected progress, in terms of numerical data and SATs results and to provide proof of this to external bodies such as Ofsted.

There is understandable concern about how such progress could be measured if pupils are given greater autonomy in their learning, creating hesitancy to move away from traditional teaching methods. Schools may find reassurance in the familiarity of formal approaches, particularly as they approach SATs. The system is deeply ingrained in ensuring all children are pushed through a uniform process by the end of primary school, making it challenging for schools to adopt innovative methods like continuous provision, even if these could potentially offer significant benefits.

How, then, can we gather evidence of the learning that takes place through this approach? Currently, most evidence comes from numerical data derived from testing and book scrutiny across various subjects. However, the nature of continuous provision shifts away from traditional methods, such as exercise books and worksheets, making anecdotal evidence and photographs more suitable. While this might initially seem daunting, particularly given teacher workload concerns, it could actually alleviate pressure by replacing marking – a task that many teachers report spending too much time on. This reclaimed time can greatly enhance teacher well-being, improve retention rates and most importantly, elevate the quality of lessons by allowing educators to focus more on identifying next steps and planning for meaningful growth in their students' learning based on observations made during lesson time.

To save even more time, older pupils could take ownership of documenting their learning by maintaining personal learning journeys. These could include their findings, reflections and progress. When it comes to providing feedback, marking is often an ineffective method for primary-aged pupils. Feedback, in a verbal, visual or demonstrative form is far more impactful when delivered in the moment, with immediate guidance on next steps while the child is still engaged in the activity.

Taking books home to mark is largely unproductive, as it has little to no effect on children's learning outcomes. Instead, it serves as evidence for other professionals to confirm that a teacher has monitored the work and suggested next steps. One of the most frustrating and time-wasting tasks I encountered in my teaching career was being required to write "verbal feedback given", sign and date each piece of work. This practice benefits no one.

When feedback is timely and meaningful, its impact is clearly reflected in a child's progress. The primary focus should be on actions that genuinely enhance learning, rather than on administrative tasks that add little value. Continuous provision has the potential to facilitate this shift.

The nature of continuous provision allows teachers to provide real-time feedback by freeing them from the need to sit and guide (or, in some cases, hand-hold) small groups. Instead, teachers can move around the classroom, observing and interacting with pupils as they engage in tasks on an individual level. At these moments, children are often in a state of "flow" – fully immersed and highly receptive to new learning. Providing immediate feedback during this optimal state not only helps to embed or extend their learning but also makes it more likely to "stick".

This type of feedback is inherently more relevant and effective because it is immediate, addressing the child's needs at the moment of learning. It is also more personalised, offering the right level of challenge or support exactly when it's needed. Through conversational engagement, teachers can gauge a pupil's understanding and adapt their guidance accordingly.

In contrast, written feedback, such as marking, often fails to pinpoint or accurately reflect the next steps a child needs to take. Even when next steps are included there is then the pressure to ensure this is received and acted upon by the child who will most probably no longer be in the right mindset for this to make any impact on their future learning. Additionally, in a busy classroom environment, teachers may prioritise supporting children who are struggling to meet objectives, leaving less time to challenge those ready to progress further. Continuous provision addresses this imbalance by creating an environment where all learners can receive the support, or challenge, they need to stretch themselves and reach their full potential.

A Way to Encourage "flow"

With this method, there is a clearer focus on the learning process rather than solely on the learning outcome. This approach enhances the effectiveness of learning by helping children understand the connections between their actions and the results they produce. For example, by exploring cause and effect, such as how changing a word can alter the mood of a piece of writing or how using shorter sentences builds suspense in a story, children develop a more nuanced understanding of the subject matter.

Focusing on the process encourages critical thinking, as pupils are required to evaluate their choices, experiment with alternatives and observe the impact of their decisions. This not only deepens their understanding of specific skills, such as crafting a narrative, but also equips them with broader problem-solving abilities. They begin to see learning as a dynamic and iterative journey, where mistakes and revisions are valuable opportunities for growth.

Additionally, this method nurtures creativity and independence. By emphasising the "how" and "why" of learning, children are encouraged to experiment and take risks, knowing that the process itself is as important as the outcome. It opens up opportunities to surprise themselves with what they can achieve through the freedom to experiment and have fun while doing so. It takes the "sting" away from making mistakes.

This focus on the process also fosters metacognitive skills, as children reflect on their learning journey and become more aware of their strategies and thinking patterns. Over time, this builds their confidence and ability to apply these strategies to new contexts, making their learning more meaningful and transferable.

Ultimately, the method of continuous provision shifts the emphasis from achieving a predefined result to fostering a deeper, more authentic engagement with the subject, which leads to more enduring and impactful learning.

It would appear then, that when considering how to introduce more opportunities for "flow" to happen in the classroom, we can begin by adopting a method such as continuous provision in all primary school classrooms – albeit a balanced form to ensure breadth of subject and skill coverage. Although implementing continuous provision further up the school would require change in classroom planning, resourcing and mindset, the potential benefits could be significant. By creating a more flexible, responsive and child-centred learning environment, this method has the power to transform primary education, offering a richer and more fulfilling experience for both pupils and educators. It represents a step towards a system where creativity, flow and meaningful learning take precedence over rigid, outcome-driven approaches, ultimately equipping children with the skills and confidence to thrive in a rapidly changing world.

References

Luton, F. (2018, April 10). *Continuous provision: From early years to year 6*. [online] Scholastic Resource Bank. Available at: https://resource-bank.scholastic.co.uk/content/Continuous-provision-from-Early-Years-to-Year-6-36254.

McHugh, K. (2024). *What is continuous provision?* [online] Early Excellence. Available at: https://earlyexcellence.com/practice-and-pedagogy/using-continuous-provision/ [Accessed 5 June 2025].

Rosen, M. (2024, June 12). *This year's KS2 Grammar, punctuation and spelling test - analysed*. [online] Blogspot.com. Available at: https://michaelrosenblog.blogspot.com/2024/06/this-years-ks2-grammar-punctuation-and.html [Accessed 15 Jan. 2025].

Severs, A. (2024, October 8). *Case study: Continuous provision and EYFS-inspired practice in KS2*. [online] Aidan Severs Consulting. Available at: https://www.aidansevers.com/post/case-study-continuous-provision-and-eyfs-inspired-practice-in-ks2 [Accessed 15 Jan. 2025].

10 Planning for "Flow"

A less rigid curriculum leaves more scope and creativity for planning, and I think it is important for teachers to be able to plan in a way that works for them. Throughout my teaching career, there was always a particular format that had to be used for planning which often differed per subject and certainly differed between schools. When we consider the relevance and importance of this in terms of outcome for the children, it really has little to no impact on the children's overall learning experience and so it is absurd that any emphasis at all is placed upon something such as this. I had the opportunity to work in a school where, for a brief period (around a year) we were encouraged to take a freer, more creative approach to our planning. We would choose a text or topic and build all our planning around it for several weeks before moving on to the next. I found it very freeing and far more enjoyable to plan using a spider diagram method. I worked alongside two other teachers in parallel classes at the time which meant that it was great for sharing and brainstorming ideas. One topic that sticks with me from that time was a topic on the moon landings. This is such a significant time in History that offers a great deal of tangible artefacts and evidence which in turn help to enthuse and engage children and yet it is something that generally is not covered by the current curriculum – what a shame! The subjects that we managed to get out of just this one topic included History, English, Art, Science, Geography and D.T. Even a little bit of Maths, in the form of measure, would have been involved throughout the topic too. I remember how we talked about the footprints left on the moon by the astronauts and how they were still visible. This led onto a discussion about weather and what the atmosphere is like on the moon. This later fed into a collaborative art lesson where we rolled out a thin layer of clay and got the children to create their own footprints which we

Teaching for Flow

mounted on the wall along with the written work they had produced about the moon landings. There was in fact so much we could do with this topic from making water-filled rockets and blasting them into the air with bicycle pumps to creating some wonderful, imaginative list poems about what might be found in an astronaut's pocket. This was so much fun and is a topic that particularly sticks with me because of the freedom myself and my colleagues had to make it a fun and engaging learning experience for all of the children.

Another example that sticks in my mind was when I chose to create an English topic of work centred around the Philip Pullman book "The Firework Maker's Daughter". I chose this because I wanted to create a link to Bonfire Night, as it aligned with the time of year I was planning for, and I had come across a wonderful story that I knew would inspire the children to write more creatively. There were so many text types we could get out of it with some imagination and creativity such as poetry, persuasive writing in the form of adverts, letters as if from the main characters, storytelling, story writing and of course reading and vocabulary work. It felt as if we had squeezed every last drop out of that text in an enjoyable and celebratory way.

The only thing missing with these examples was the child-led element. These ideas and activities were still very much teacher driven and while there would almost certainly have been "flow" happening at times for most children, we most probably would not have reached the optimum point for "flow" to happen effortlessly on a daily basis. So how do we do that?

A huge part of doing this well is going to be down to the relationship that is built between the teacher and the children in the class. Through this relationship, the teacher will already have some idea of what interests the children have and what really engages them, but this can only guide us so far. We also know that interests will differ greatly within a class dynamic and so where do we even begin?

Currently, the standard approach when we begin a topic is that we already have a clear sense of what objectives we are going to teach and what learning we want the children to get out of it each session building up to ticking off a whole predetermined list of objectives by the end of the topic or unit of work. Often, we will begin a topic by establishing what the children already know so that we know where to focus more of our teaching time. Supposing, instead of asking the children what they already know and getting them to record this, we ask them what they would like to know. Instead of planning every step and having a list of objectives to cover we could start with a provocative question or scenario and let the pupils' curiosity guide the sessions.

Let's take the example topic of the moon landings. In this example, we could begin by asking the pupils what they would like to know about space exploration. Inviting them to pose questions either in writing or spoken word we could use this to guide the planning, leading to more personal investment and potentially more opportunities for "flow" to occur for each pupil within the topic. With more able or older pupils, I'm thinking year five and year six, giving them ownership over the topic with a project-based learning approach could offer the freedom they need to enter a state of "flow". This approach would involve allowing pupils to explore a topic over an extended period, ending with a tangible product or presentation. The process becomes more student driven as they research, collaborate and create based on their interests within the topic. A project like building a model of the solar system or creating a short film about the moon could provide the space for "flow" to emerge naturally, with students driving their own learning. However, this approach can take a fair amount of training and having been a teacher, I know that this approach is not going to necessarily be suitable for all within a cohort. Some children naturally need more structured adult input. In these cases, a learning station and choice board approach could be really beneficial. It is still really important, even when introducing structure, that the element of choice remains to allow for that ownership over the task and enhance motivation. By providing a variety of activities or stations, where students can choose what they want to explore next, can help foster autonomy. I imagine this to look similar to continuous provision in the Early Years (please refer to the chapter on continuous provision to learn more about this). For example, after reading the first few pages of *The Firework Maker's Daughter* where Lila grows up learning how to make fireworks with her father you could set up various activities that link to firework making such as a firework art task, a science experiment linked to fireworks, fact files, PowerPoint presentations or explanation texts about fireworks, etc. or perhaps more realistically you may decide to focus your teaching on something you have assessed that the children need to work on. It could be around looking at the language of the text together, what adjectives are used? Are there any examples of powerful verbs? Can you think of any others we could use? Use the children's ideas to add ideas to a working wall. Once you have done your focused teaching input there could be a number of activities that the children can choose from that could build on this teaching, allowing them to apply and experiment with the knowledge and skills they have been taught.

I find it best to display my ideas in a spider diagram model as seen below (Figure 10.1):

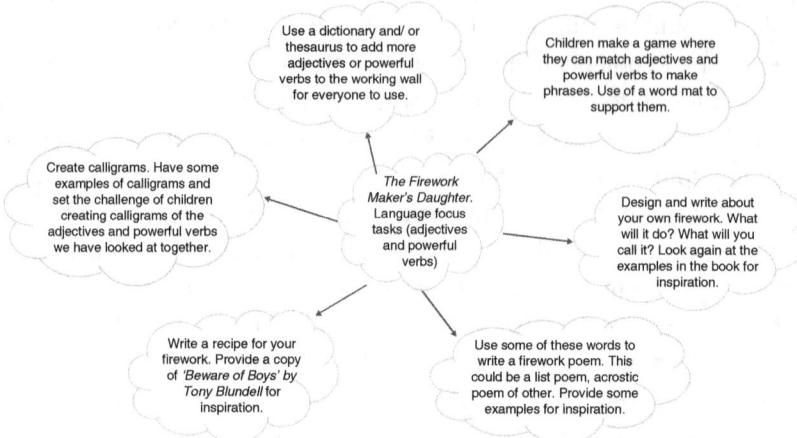

Figure 10.1 An example of planning, depicting a unit of work on language focus centring around the book, *The Firework Maker's Daughter* by Philip Pullman.

Essentially, variety and choice are needed to create a learning environment that fosters opportunities for "flow" to happen.

The Subject of Mathematics

How could this approach work in a subject such as Maths? Maths is a particular subject which is often stand-alone within the curriculum where we are used to working through a structured programme of learning. Where in the past many schools used schemes such as "Abacus", today many schools use online schemes of work such as "White Rose Maths". The teaching of maths has moved increasingly towards the use of models and images to help children gain a better overall understanding of the strategies and methods used to solve an equation, yet it still seems to me that children generally find it difficult to apply this to real-life mathematical problems or puzzles. They simply struggle to make the connection between the learning that happens in a maths lesson and how or when they practically apply it. I suppose we have to ask ourselves, why are we still teaching maths in a way that is fairly stand-alone? Is this really the only way? Most importantly, is it the most effective way? I have heard many people refer to having a "fear of maths". I used to very much have this until I became a teacher and have always put it

Planning for "Flow"

down to the nature of maths as having either a "right" or a "wrong" answer. Even now if someone asks me to man a stall, I have a slight wave of panic about having to give change, even though I know full well I can work it out quite easily now. This is described by some as "maths anxiety".

Research conducted by the University of Cambridge revealed some interesting insights into maths anxiety. Contrary to the assumption that it primarily affects pupils with additional learning needs, the findings showed that even cognitively able pupils often experience maths anxiety. In many cases, this anxiety emerged first and then began to negatively impact their performance over time, creating a self-perpetuating cycle of stress and underachievement. But what causes this anxiety to occur in the first place? The study attempted to look into the cause. Some of its findings are stated below:

> More detailed investigation in 1,700 UK schoolchildren found that a general feeling that maths was more difficult than other subjects often contributed to maths anxiety, leading to a lack or loss of confidence. Students pointed to poor marks or test results, or negative comparisons to peers or siblings as reasons for feeling anxious.
>
> (Szucs, 2019)

It also mentioned how maths anxiety is more prevalent in girls compared to boys. It would appear that this is having an overall impact on society as a whole too according to the Centre for Neurological Science:

> Taking maths as an example again – despite really small differences being seen in terms of performance at school, women are poorly represented in the job market after university, with 94% of maths professors in the UK being men, according to a survey commissioned by the London Mathematical Society.
>
> (Centre for Educational Neuroscience, 2016)

Could some of this be down to stereotyping or "pigeon holing"? This is something that many of us do in various ways that affects how we view ourselves and others in terms of ability whether consciously or unconsciously. Could the way we teach mathematics in our schools be exacerbating the problem? At the very least, is there something we can change about the way we teach it that may lessen the impact, particularly for girls? One thing that does seem to be clear to me is that many of the maths lessons we teach in schools seem detached from "real life" experience. If something feels detached from real life it is hard to see its true purpose or worth.

Children should still have the opportunity to learn through role play. For example, in a shop where they can experience adding coins and giving change. Many children these days are so unfamiliar with coins and notes – they do not get the opportunity to pay in real-life contexts with physical money as paying by card or using an app on your phone is now the social norm. We need to find relevant ways for our modern-day pupils to explore maths in a practical and fun way that does not always require them to work from or directly onto a worksheet. Some ideas that come to mind are the following:

- Using those combination padlocks to create a fun and practical problem-solving session where the children must solve the mathematical problems in order to work out the correct combination on the lock to open it.
- Role play – This could be dependent on the maths topic. It could be a shop to practice addition of money and coins or perhaps a bank or finding ways for this to be done digitally. If the topic is measurement the role play could be builder's yard or a "be an architect for a day" themed day where they could practise measuring various lengths or even a chef's kitchen, e.g. where they could measure in grams, kilograms, litres and millilitres.
- Custom-made board/dice/card games – these could even be designed and made by the children. They could all have a go at playing each other's games creating even more learning opportunities.
- Maths treasure hunts/trails/orienteering activities where each clue requires you to solve a mathematical problem to get to the next location. For example, they might need to solve a series of division problems which relate to letters in a given key, spelling out the next location.
- Creating maths puzzles, problems, riddles or word problems to share with "pen pal mathematicians" from another school. This could be a regular activity perhaps once a month or once a term where pupils challenge each other on various maths topics.

It's important to give purpose to maths. Far too often maths seems detached from real life and leaves children questioning why do I need to know this? I think this is partly down to breaking it down into small manageable steps focusing on strategies and methods of how to solve mathematical equations. But there appears to be so much focus on learning the mechanics and very little on the real-life application. One of the problems with learning step-by-step approaches without the real-life application part is that students do not gain a full understanding of what it is they are doing or why they are doing it. This can lead to misremembered rules and difficulty in applying the maths when they need it.

In the Netherlands, an instruction theory for the teaching of mathematics has been developed known as Realistic Mathematics Education (RME). RME is about teaching Maths through a context-based approach which can be based on real-life scenarios or could even be fictional such as a concept linked to a fairy tale. Ideally it needs to be something that the students can relate to and get on board with. The lessons take on a more "active" nature where the students learn not just the formula to solve their maths equation but allows them to gain a full understanding of the connections that lead to getting the final answer.

> The researchers found that Dutch students – taught using RME – were not only more accurate when solving division problems, they were also more confident about their methods. The English students made more errors and reporting being less certain about what they were doing.
> (Realistic Maths Education, n.d.)

This has proved to be a very effective way of teaching mathematics and demonstrates how important it is for children to gain a good understanding of the why and how of using methods so that they are able to make connections, apply what they have already learned effectively, and problem-solve in a variety of situations. I thought it was particularly interesting that the children who were taught using the RME method were noticeably more confident in their approach to mathematical problems compared with their English counterparts.

Topics Rather Than Subjects

We tend to teach via individual subjects with little overlap or at least little attention is drawn to any connection between subjects with perhaps the exception of ICT. Maybe, in order to build stronger connections and make a subject seem relevant and purposeful we need to move away from stand-alone subjects with the emphasis being on the skills needed to learn about a particular topic rather than subject. As an example, let's take a popular topic with

Teaching for Flow

children such as dinosaurs. What might our planning for this topic look like that will ensure we are covering a range of subjects, teaching relevant skills and imparting useful knowledge? Clearly, as we touched on earlier, a good starting point is to gauge the children's interests around the subject and ask them what they want to know or find out more about the topic but here are a few different ideas of what could get you started.

Table 10.1 A plan to demonstrate how we can use a topic to span and connect a range of subjects and skill sets covered

Topic – Dinosaurs	
Facts and history	**Fossils**
Find out about any local history that may exist related to dinosaurs. Visit a museum. Research and record facts about dinosaurs in different ways including written fact files, video clips (which could be "David Attenborough style"), presentations, etc. Design a dinosaur museum for other classes and even parents to come and visit with facts, models, artwork of landscapes (these could be layered pictures similar to the rainforest artwork by Henry Rousseau), fossils etc.	How are they formed? Learn about palaeontology and famous people e.g. Mary Anning Create own fossils by pressing objects into clay or plaster. Go on a trip to do some fossil hunting or set up an outdoor activity where children can dig for "fossil models" and learn about the process.
Sound	**Moving models**
Explore sounds of dinosaurs – the Natural History Museum website is good for this. Recreate sounds with instruments. Have a go at making instruments that make "dinosaur" sounds. Learn about pitch and tone. Learn about vibrations. Learn songs about dinosaurs.	Learn about air pressure and pneumatics to create a dinosaur that moves in some way e.g. tongue sticks out, breathes, pops up etc. (I highly recommend the book: *Moving Monsters* by Lynn Huggins-Cooper.)

(Continued)

Planning for "Flow"

Table 10.1 (Continued)

Topic – Dinosaurs	
Animals	**Story telling**
Learn about animal groups and where dinosaurs fit in.	Read and share stories about dinosaurs
Diet of dinosaurs.	Learn the difference between fact and fiction.
Habitat – include a bit of Geography and Climate in here.	Create, tell and write stories about dinosaurs.
Skeletons and naming bones in the body.	Perform shadow puppet shows involving dinosaurs.
Examine footprints of different animals and measure and compare them.	Stop-go-animations using dinosaur toys.
Subjects covered: Science, History, Music, English, Design and Technology, Art, Maths, Geography and ICT.	
Developing skills: creativity and creative thinking, presentation, problem-solving, planning, collaboration, researching, organising information, gross and fine motor skills, sequencing, fact recall.	

This example illustrates how we can plan for learning to be more relevant and purposeful by moving away from isolated subjects and instead focusing on teaching a broad set of skills through engaging topics that interest the current cohort of children, like dinosaurs. This method emphasises cross-subject connections, allowing children to explore their interests while developing essential skills and knowledge. The examples such as "creating a museum" are particularly powerful in the way that they offer children the opportunity to all add their individual piece of work towards a shared goal creating purposeful engagement and ultimately a sense of achievement for each individual.

Planning on the Go

It is important to emphasise that this style of planning is and should be merely ideas that you can draw from as and when needed within the teaching of the topic. This is because for "flow" to have an even greater prospect of happening we need to adopt a more "planning in the moment" approach where we are guided by the developing outcomes as they unfold within the class dynamic.

I first learned about "planning in the moment" when I was introduced to the work of Anna Ephgrave. In short, her work centres around the idea that early years practitioners look for "the teachable moments" that open up and present themselves while children are engaged in their play. This is done through clever use of questioning and finding ways to extend the learning through the setting up of further opportunities within the classroom setting.

> ... a skilful adult will spot a "teachable moment". They then decide what to do – this is the planning. They might provide an extra resource, an idea, some vocabulary, some information, or they might model a skill or demonstrate how to use a piece of equipment – this is teaching.
>
> (Ephgrave, 2020, p. 112)

Although Anna Ephgrave's approach is aimed at children in the early years I believe that there is relevance to this approach as we move away from a restrictive curriculum. I also wonder whether this is a healthier approach to planning in general.

One drawback to "planning in the moment" could be resourcing in terms of ensuring that there is a wide range of suitable resources available for the children to use at any given time. This, of course, costs money and with funding being an ever-increasing issue this could well be a hindrance to the effective implementation of "planning in the moment". There are, however, some ways around this by considering reusing and recycling, donations, making more use of the outdoor environment and what it has to offer, homemade resources such as salt dough and resource sharing and swapping across schools within a partnership.

A common question that arises when considering a less prescriptive, more flexible approach to education (particularly from educators and professionals accustomed to traditional methods) is: In a child-led learning model, how do we ensure that children are taught everything they need to know? Naomi Fisher, author of *A Different Way to Learn*, addresses this concern effectively in her book. She argues how traditional schooling does not guarantee that all children learn what they need to know. She states:

> Many young people leave school without the basic skills they need and without any idea of how to acquire these for themselves.

> Self-directed children do all learn different things, although they will develop some of the same skills, particularly skills which are important in our society such as reading.
>
> (Fisher, 2023, p. 98)

This perspective challenges the long-standing assumption that traditional schooling is the only way to ensure children acquire necessary knowledge and skills. Instead, it invites us to reconsider the purpose of education and the ways in which learning happens.

A child-led approach recognises that learning is not a one-size-fits-all process. It allows children to develop at their own pace, following their interests and passions, which (as we've looked at previously) can lead to deeper engagement and intrinsic motivation. For example, a child fascinated by nature might develop scientific inquiry skills through exploring ecosystems, while another captivated by storytelling might hone language and communication skills through avid reading and creative writing.

Of course, this approach raises valid concerns about ensuring that children are exposed to a broad range of knowledge. One way to address this is by creating rich, resource-filled environments that inspire curiosity and exploration. However, adult input is also crucial in planting seeds of interest and steering learning pathways. Parents and educators must work together when it comes to observing children's interests, gently introducing new ideas, and facilitating opportunities to expand their learning horizons wherever possible.

Ultimately, Fisher's argument reminds us that no educational approach can guarantee comprehensive knowledge acquisition for all children. What we can strive for, however, is fostering adaptable, curious and resourceful individuals who are equipped to learn to independently and confidently navigate the world.

Having read Naomi Fischer's work and the knowledge I have gained, it is evident that neurodivergent children could benefit enormously from a "planning on the go" approach. Another common concern that may arise is whether this approach is suitable only for neurodivergent children, and what about neurotypical children? In my view, neurotypical children would benefit just as much from this approach. The current structure of our education system, which often spoon-feeds knowledge and skills, may actually limit the thought processes and learning opportunities that would otherwise naturally emerge for all children.

I've frequently heard that high-achieving students, while excelling academically, can sometimes struggle with practical decision-making or common sense. This suggests that a prescriptive approach may hinder their ability to think critically and problem-solve independently. By being too directive, we prevent children from discovering solutions on their own and learning from trial, error and mistakes – key elements in developing strategies for lifelong learning.

When we do too much for them, such as focusing on test preparation or correcting mistakes ourselves instead of letting them find and address errors, it can unintentionally stifle their independence. In trying to help, we may inadvertently disable their capacity for self-directed learning when we should be fostering it.

The Possible Impact on the Mental Health of Teachers

After educating myself on a little cognitive behavioural therapy (CBT), I have learned that unhelpful thinking styles such as "what if" thinking can enter you into a cycle of anxiety. When we consider the current way in which we plan, we are often encouraged to consider all of the possible "what if" outcomes to ensure that we are as prepared as we can be for what may take place in the lesson. We are trying to predict the future which in itself is impossible, things will occur that we won't have and could not have planned for. The result of which leaves us with the feeling that that lesson did not go well and leads us to the "should have" way of thinking which is equally damaging as a thought process. Often, things will happen in the daily life of a classroom that are completely out of your control, yet as teachers I believe that we are conditioned to view this as completely our own responsibility and leads to us blaming ourselves and feeling the weight of what may have not gone the way we had planned. When we are observed in a lesson, we are scrutinised for all aspects of that one lesson. If something "unexpected" happens within that observed lesson, although it may be acknowledged that the "unexpected" thing was an anomaly we will often be encouraged to consider what we would do should this occur again. The more experience you gain as a teacher, the more "what if" scenarios you are likely to need to consider. This thinking style is similar to personalisation (where a person may blame themselves for something outside of their control) which is another unhelpful thinking style that leads to poor mental health. It seems unsurprising that this could then lead to increasing sense of overwhelm and ultimately burn out.

If we compare the traditional forms of planning with a "planning in the moment" approach, in the view of whether or not it is better for our mental health, it seems that it would be rather beneficial. While planning for the future, we are bound to come up with many ideas that are merely hypothetical, meaning that teachers are wasting precious time and energy planning for something that may or may not happen. Not only that but this way of thinking is bad for our mental health. Constant dwelling on hypothetical scenarios can lead to overthinking, stress and anxiety. During the school day there are numerous things that can happen that can change the course of action in practice. A few examples could include pupil sickness, unexpected changes to timetabling, technical issues, friendship fallouts and even difficulties in a pupil's home life filtering into the classroom. In these moments, teachers have to be flexible and work effectively prioritising the biggest need in that circumstance. This demonstrates that teachers already have the skills to adapt and change effectively within the moment. Imagine if the majority of our planning was "in the moment". There would be less "wasted" and unproductive time spent before lessons and fewer missed learning opportunities during the learning journey as you flexibly adapt as you go extending learning through careful questioning, and open ended and investigatory tasks. It would also empower teachers to exercise their professional judgement more freely when assessing students and planning their next steps. Planning could even become a process that involves the children rather than something that is done solely by the teacher behind closed doors. Involving the pupils in the planning process regularly could be a fantastic way to engage them and make their learning journey more meaningful.

Grasping the Teachable Moments

It often seems as if schools limit themselves when it comes to leaning into learning opportunities that present themselves due to the backlash they fear they may be faced with from senior staff or sometimes from parents. Unfortunately, a culture of "teacher bashing" persists, often exacerbated by the limited support and protection teachers receive from the government and external agencies. This is further compounded by the lack of authority afforded to them to effectively manage the consequences that arise. The result of which leads to schools making "safe choices" in an attempt to avoid any repercussions but ultimately impedes them in making the right decisions in terms of educational benefits. A clear example of this became apparent to me very recently when my very excited daughter skipped off to school in an unexpected flurry of snow equipped with Wellington boots and warm clothing. Somewhat disappointingly, we received an email from the headteacher that same day explaining that they would keep the children from playing in the snow on this occasion but that next time they could bring in wellies and a change of clothes to play in it. While I understand that children's safety is paramount, I also felt there were ways around this and that a valuable learning opportunity had been missed – one that may not come around again for quite some time, especially given our increasingly unpredictable climate. All children bring P.E. kit to school on a Monday and keep it there until a Friday meaning that they all have a change of clean dry clothes and spare shoes should they have gotten too wet in the snow. Some schools ask the children to bring in a pair of wellies to keep in school to use every day of the year. A consideration may be a change to uniform policies. Controversially, I'd much rather children came to school dressed appropriately for the weather conditions to allow more outdoor activities to take place as and when the moment arises than for parents to have to fork out on expensive garments with the school logo on. Surely the benefits that the children would have gained from playing in the snow would far outweigh any risk. They could have developed their teamwork skills, creativity, understanding of cause and effect, learning about freezing and melting, being immersed in a whole sensory experience and building their resilience by being out in the cold weather. The risks would be minimal – they might get wet and cold, or worst case they might slip and hurt themselves.

Admittedly, this approach to planning may take some getting used to, with a move away from following schemes of work and the implementation of a more creative planning style which could take up valuable time initially. However, teachers are extremely resourceful and expert in sharing innovative ideas that have worked well in their classrooms and so with shared input and the freedom to experiment and plan in a way that is fitting for their classes, it wouldn't take long before teachers began to establish a rhythm with this style of planning. Over time, the benefits of this approach can outweigh the initial investment in terms of planning time. As teachers collaborate and exchange successful methods, they can build a shared library of cross-curricular resources, activities and strategies that enrich the learning experience. This approach not only fosters professional growth but also allows teachers to be more responsive to their students' evolving interests and needs.

Moreover, allowing flexibility in planning encourages teachers to tailor lessons in a way that aligns with their unique teaching styles and their students' preferred ways of learning. As teachers experiment with themes that spark curiosity, they are better placed to engage students deeply, making learning more impactful and memorable.

In practice, this shift could also reduce teacher burnout by breaking up repetitive planning cycles and providing opportunities to explore new, innovative approaches each year. Due to the interconnecting nature of planning in themes, it is possible that it takes up less brain space than when you are having to plan for each individual subject on a different topic. When teachers feel empowered to design lessons around broad, interconnected topics, they're more likely to experience professional satisfaction, fostering a positive classroom environment where curiosity and creativity thrive.

Ultimately, this planning approach places value on the teaching process itself, encouraging both teachers and pupils to find joy in discovery, connect knowledge across subjects and engage meaningfully with each lesson.

References

Centre for Educational Neuroscience. (2016). *Girls and boys have different cognitive abilities*. [online] Centre for Educational Neuroscience. Available at: https://www.educationalneuroscience.org.uk/resources/neuromyth-or-neurofact/girls-and-boys-have-different-cognitive-abilities/ [Accessed 5 June 2025].

Ephgrave, A. (2020). *Planning in the Moment with Two and Three Year Olds: Child-Initiated Play in Action*. Routledge.

Fisher, N. (2023). *A Different Way to Learn*. Jessica Kingsley Publishers.

Realistic Maths Education. (n.d.). *What does research say about RME?* [online] RME. Available at: https://rme.org.uk/what-is-rme/research-on-rme/ [Accessed 5 June 2025].

Szucs, D. (2019, March 14). *Report examines origins and nature of 'maths anxiety'*. [online] University of Cambridge. Available at: https://www.cam.ac.uk/research/news/report-examines-origins-and-nature-of-maths-anxiety [Accessed 5 June 2025].

 Meaningful Assessment
Focusing on the Whole Child

There are many forms of assessment, but it seems that those forms that produce numerical data take precedence over the rest. This is all well and good as you can see clear differences when comparing data from all sections of society and can use this to produce graphs, league tables and see rises and falls in performance. Nevertheless, the problem with numerical data is that it can be falsified or manipulated and does not always give a full, rounded picture of the reality in every given situation. It also assumes that we can measure the success of all in the same way. It assumes a one-size-fits-all model which of course is not and can never be realistic. Quite frankly, it is damaging when it comes to self-esteem and productivity.

Let's compare, for the moment, two very different famous people who are extremely able and excel in their field. The first being Stephen Wiltshire, a British artist who has the ability to draw incredibly detailed city landscapes from memory. As a child, Stephen was non-verbal and diagnosed with autism. It was clear however, that he had a real talent for art and this was a form of communication to him. By the age of just eight years old he had received a commission from the Prime Minister for a drawing of Salisbury Cathedral. Today, he is a world-renowned artist and has received an MBE for his services to art.

Now compare this to the very talented Beth Tweddle, arguably Britain's best female gymnast. Beth began gymnastics at the age of seven and within a short space of time had begun to be recognised for her talent. She also completed a degree in sports science alongside pursuing her gymnastics career.

So here we have two very talented children of primary school age, specifically the beginning of key stage two when their talents were already beginning to be recognised. The opportunities they had been given during

Meaningful Assessment: Focusing on the Whole Child

this time to explore, practise and grow their interest and talent were perhaps crucial to their future success. Now imagine asking these two people, as children of primary school age, to sit the exact same test, the result of which placing them into a category of exceeding expectations, meeting expectations or working towards or below expectations. Bearing in mind that the test given would be neither in art and design nor in gymnastics but in mathematics, writing, reading or spelling and grammar. Would the information that was gained from these tests tell us everything we need to know about the ability and potential of these pupils, the quality of teaching or the opportunities presented to the children? If we think about the ability and potential of the pupils first, in these two cases both were extremely talented and went on to accomplish great things but their particular talents in the areas they excelled in would not have been recognised in standard academic testing at primary level. It seems clear from these examples that a single test cannot provide a holistic view of a child's full potential. It is unknown to me how both of these people, in particular, performed in other subjects while at primary level but regardless I think it shows that it is essentially meaningless.

During my time as a teacher, I taught a child who, similarly to Stephen was diagnosed with autism and was non-verbal when she began her primary school years but in addition she was brought up as bilingual understanding both English and Chinese. Initially, she would make noises and scream in an attempt to communicate. Similarly to Stephen she also had a talent in art. She would draw fantastic cartoon pictures of both familiar children's TV characters from CBeebies such as Bing and Boj but would also invent her own. She would even create really clear images of characters out of loose items that she could find around the classroom. More often than not she would choose to draw on whiteboards which was a little bit problematic if they got wiped by accident and so we provided her with a special art book. In an attempt to encourage her to communicate more using her words, myself and a fantastic teaching assistant, who later went on to train to become a teacher, decided to pop her art book up on a high shelf to encourage her to ask for it. This started off with gentle encouragement to use the word "book". This slowly grew to "art book", followed by "art book, please" until she could use the whole sentence "Mrs Meager, Can I have my art book, please?". I'll never forget the first time she went up to another teacher on the playground, used their name and said "look there's a plane!" The progress that this child had made was incredible, however the way her brain worked and the way she learned left her unable to access the standard tests at the end of key stage one. Alternative assessment arrangements were made for her, but this meant that the progress we had recorded as a school was not recognised in league tables or anywhere outside of this school – essentially, to my mind, written off.

In terms of the quality of teaching, the tests do not highlight some really important development points such as the success of children's teachers in helping them to progress in their communication skills by using their enthusiasm for other subjects such as art as an incentive. This demonstrates that so many cases of fantastic, effective teaching and learning cannot be measured numerically, and I feel that it is a shame that we are missing a huge chunk of the picture. In fact, the current way of assessing gives us very little information on the impact that the teachers of both Beth and Stephen had on their future outcomes. The fact that their potential was recognised at a young age suggests they were given the necessary opportunities needed to flourish – be that in school or out of school. Yet, the testing system would give us absolutely no indication of this whatsoever. With this in mind, it makes you wonder how accurate a picture is this numerical data creating? Data that so much emphasis is placed upon! It begs the question, what realistic conclusions can be drawn of not just the overall performance of pupils but of the quality of teachers and schools as a whole – not just in the core subjects?

Gathering information using the standardised tests cannot possibly build a solid enough picture when it only measures the pupil's attainment in one particular topic, on one particular day. As teachers, we've all had those pupils who have not performed as well as expected on the day or even those who have managed to tick the right boxes but we know from day-to-day lessons that their score does not truly reflect their current attainment.

Pigeonholing

As teachers, we often subconsciously "pigeonhole" students, placing them into categories and groups based on our perceptions of their abilities. Most of the time, we do this without even realising it. However, these classifications can subtly shape our expectations of students, influencing how we interact with them and, in turn, how they perceive themselves as learners. The messages we send, whether intentionally or not, can have a lasting impact on a child's confidence, self-worth and approach to learning.

This tendency is largely driven by the way education systems are structured. Teachers are conditioned to prepare children for the next test, the next assessment, or the next set of targets. Before a lesson even begins, we have often already determined which students will require a differentiated version of the work and have prepared it accordingly. While this is informed by prior knowledge of the students, it also reinforces fixed perceptions about their abilities. By doing so, we may unintentionally limit their potential, failing to recognise the full scope of what they are capable of achieving.

It is crucial that we remain open to truly "seeing" our students – beyond the labels, categories and preconceptions. We must never assume that a child's current level of performance defines their future potential. History offers numerous examples of highly successful individuals who were underestimated during their school years.

Take Roald Dahl, for example, one of the most beloved children's authors of all time. His school reports described him as "indolent and illiterate", a judgement he later reflected on in a 1979 episode of *Desert Island Discs*, still available on BBC Sounds. Albert Einstein, one of the most influential theoretical physicists in history, was reportedly told by a teacher that he would "never amount to anything". Winston Churchill, widely regarded as one of the greatest political figures of all time, received poor school reports, yet his leadership left an indelible mark on history. John Lennon, the legendary musician and songwriter, was another student who received discouraging feedback from teachers but went on to shape the music industry in profound ways.

What is striking about these individuals is that formal schooling did not necessarily play a key role in nurturing their talents. Instead, their success was driven by passion, determination and an ability to find their own "flow". This raises an important question: How many children throughout history have been held back by an education system that failed to recognise or support their true potential? Unfortunately, this is a question we may never be able to answer.

Perhaps the issue lies in the traditional model of passive learning. By this I refer to sitting at desks, absorbing information and conforming to rigid structures. For individuals like Dahl, Einstein, Churchill and Lennon, this model was inherently at odds with their creative and inquisitive natures. Had they been given more autonomy, more opportunities to engage in active learning, and more freedom to explore their interests, their school experiences might have been vastly different.

While we cannot change the past, we can shape the future. As educators, we must challenge our own biases and remain open to the limitless potential within each child. By fostering an environment where students feel seen, valued and empowered to learn in ways that suit them, we can help ensure that no child is unfairly confined by the limitations of a system that was never designed to fit all learners.

Testing Pupils or Teachers?

As I mentioned in a previous chapter, Michael Rosen is very outspoken and reassuringly on the side of teachers when it comes to testing at key stage 2. It is abundantly clear the disdain he has for the grammar, punctuation and spelling tests in particular. He says this on his blog:

> So, we test children in order to test teachers. This is a Michael Gove idea. I wonder even if this is legal! It's like punishing someone for something that someone else has done! (Meant, partly tongue in cheek.)
> (Rosen, 2024)

Some would argue that we need the numerical data to be able to compare cohorts of children against their peers not just within the school setting but also nationally. It is also true that when you go for a job, you need to share your qualifications but an employer will more than likely make their final decision based on the experience and skill that you are able to demonstrate during the interview process than whether you achieved a 9 (or in old money A*) over a 7 (or B) at GCSE, for example. Outside of a school context we're often told not to compare ourselves to others and that is not good for our mental health to constantly compare ourselves to others, yet the school system as soon as you enter into it, is centred around comparing you and your attainment to your peers. For one, this assumes we should all reach the same milestones at the same time which is just simply not realistic. We all come from different backgrounds and have different opportunities and levels of knowledge imparted to us in our home environments, before we have even started school. On average, schools in deprived areas will perform less well than schools in affluent areas.

> Just 16 per cent of schools in the most deprived areas are "outstanding", compared with 37 per cent in the least deprived.
> (Staufenberg, 2018)

It is often talked about breaking the cycle of poor attainment in deprived areas but if our system was successful in doing that then we wouldn't still be facing this issue. From experience, the parents of pupils who would be classed as "deprived" have often encountered negative experiences in school themselves and they are often the parents that you need to work harder with to build a positive and trusting relationship. It's almost as if they've been chewed up and spat out by the system, with the impact being hugely negative both in terms of their attitude towards learning and education in general and how they view themselves and their children as learners. In some cases, it may even have an impact on how they can valuably contribute to society. Not everyone can be high flying heart surgeons, but there is a role for everyone based on their individual enthusiasm and/or skill that they have a desire to pursue, which in so doing can help them gain other skills along the way.

Fundamentally, standardised testing does not celebrate nor even acknowledge any other skills, knowledge or proficiencies that are not covered by the test. If someone is not performing so well in the core subjects (maths, reading or writing) as teachers we would continue to support them but if we had a way of assessing, reporting and even showcasing what they are good at, think what that would do for each child's confidence and self-worth. I'm not saying that subjects such as English and maths are not important, I'm merely saying that pupils are more likely to want to put the effort into improving skills in these areas if they are a part of something they are more easily able to succeed in and they enjoy. It would give pupils a purpose and a set of clear goals to work towards which naturally would draw in other skills such as reading, maths and writing as they broaden their horizons and find the motivation to aim higher. For example, a child who lives and breathes football, but who struggles to read and write, may want to improve their reading skills if faced with a list of football statistics or an interview or newspaper report about a match. If they want to be able to read the match report, they are more likely to want to put the effort in than if they are faced with say another "Biff, Chip and Kipper" book which may have little to no interest for them.

Moving Away from Numerical Data

If numerical data is not the answer, then what methods of assessment would work best in highlighting the true progress and potential of the pupils and performance of each individual school? We touched briefly on what this may look like in the curriculum chapter but let's explore this in more detail.

In early years foundation stage, teachers gather evidence throughout the year through examples of work, photographs and even video clips. These are usually recorded on programmes such as "Tapestry" which is accessible to senior staff at school as well as to parents. One of the best things about this is that parents can add to it too, so if for example, a child has met a milestone of learning at home e.g. how to tie their own shoelaces or learned how to ride their bike with no stabilisers at the weekend, this can be recorded too. This type of recording process helps to build a clear picture of each individual child's development and enables teachers to effectively track a child's progress. This is valuable not only because it avoids judging a child solely on their performance in a narrow range of tasks on a single day, but also because it offers a clearer picture of how they apply their learning to real-life problems they encounter.

In 2021, however, we saw the introduction of the Reception Baseline Assessment (RBA) which are tasks involving physical equipment set for the children. These assessments must be conducted in the first six weeks of schooling. They were introduced as a starting point to measure pupils' progress throughout their primary school years. This was a controversial move as a significant number of teachers felt at the time that this would not create an accurate picture of the children's current attainment, and a large majority were concerned that it would have a negative impact on children.

> Four in five teachers did not think the baseline provided an accurate picture of children's current attainment, while 69 per cent said it had not helped develop positive relationships with pupils.
> Eighty-three per cent of teachers said it increased their workload.
> (Dickens, 2020)

Despite the professional opinion of the many teachers who had spoken out about this, the Government rolled it out anyway. It is unclear what impact this has had since its implementation other than the clear ever-increasing workload for teachers. From a professional viewpoint, it is impossible to see that any benefits would outweigh the negatives and quite frankly the implementation of such an assessment feels like a lack of trust in teacher's professional judgements. Is there truly a need for such an assessment if teachers are using an all-encompassing and ongoing system such as Tapestry anyway? The RBA only provides a snapshot of a child's abilities in literacy, communication, language and mathematics at a specific point in time. The argument is that the RBA is useful in identifying any immediate areas of support needed. This would assume that a teacher would not identify them in a timely manner otherwise. The danger is we end up focussing too heavily on the "what can't they do?" rather than the "what can they do?" right from the outset of their learning journey. This can be problematic because it can potentially create a deficit-based mindset. Children may be seen through the lens of their limitations rather than their strengths and potential. This focus might undermine their confidence and motivation to learn, as they may feel defined by what they struggle with rather than encouraged to build on their existing skills. When a designer or architect works on a new project, they work with what already exists to create a new feature that works in harmony with the environment or landscape. In a similar way, in education if we recognise the strengths and build upon them it is a far more enjoyable and positive experience that fosters growth and development.

Further up the school, end-of-term assessment papers are generally used to monitor the children's progress in phonics, reading, spelling, grammar and maths. Other various assessment systems will be in place for non-core subjects, but these core subjects are the ones that will be shared with the senior leadership team and will be scrutinised and analysed. These again, are just a snapshot of what a child can do on a particular day and teachers will often find themselves having to explain away any anomalies if perhaps a child had not performed as well as they potentially could have on that particular test. It would be far more accurate and would give a more holistic view of a pupil's overall progress to have more of an evidence-based data collection process, like that of Tapestry, as children progress through the school. The advantages of this would be that it is a child centred, accessible record that would give a comprehensive view of the child's strengths and areas for development across the wider curriculum. Furthermore, this can be seamlessly shared between schools which is vitally important when a child moves from one school to another and provides the new teacher with a more in-depth picture of the child than merely some surface-level numerical data. As a teacher, I often found that reading a child's previous report, particularly the general comments section, gave far more useful information than simply the data from previous assessments.

An information gathering approach, such as this, may raise some concerns about the workload, in that collecting the evidence would take up valuable time and add to the daily tasks a teacher needs to do. But on closer inspection, if it replaces the current assessments and is ongoing it also removes the need for written marking, lengthy progress meetings and could even replace report writing which takes up a huge amount of teacher's time and rarely benefits the children in terms of learning. Feedback about a child's work should be given verbally and, in the moment, so that it is meaningful, you can check their understanding, iron out any misconceptions and successfully move learning on. Parents would be updated consistently and regularly with access to their child's individualised progress through a system such as "Tapestry" – also allowing them to add outside of school achievements such as swimming certificates or dance grading. The system could be developed to alert teachers and senior staff to any potential drop or stagnation in progress – allowing issues to be addressed in a timely manner and not just waiting until the end of term progress reviews. I suppose what we need to ask ourselves is, is it better to have a record of what we could potentially say and do to support a child in their learning or is it better to physically see the improvement and progression that is being made through keeping an evidential record of successes?

One promising approach to assessment that Dr. Thomas Armstrong advocates is known as "ipsative" assessment. Rather than comparing students to one another (a practice that, as we have explored, can be problematic for many reasons) ipsative assessment measures progress on an individual level. This shifts the focus from competition to personal development, making assessment far more meaningful and useful for both students and teachers.

Armstrong states:

> It's time that teachers made 'ipsative' assessment (comparing a student to his past performances) a regular part of their vocabulary. This shift in emphasis would be a welcome countermeasure to the current emphasis on 'core' learning skills and standardized test scores taken as absolute values.
>
> (Armstong, 2020)

Armstrong highlights various ways this approach can be implemented. For example, in reading, a teacher might video record a child reading a book of their choice at the beginning of the year and then again at the end of the year. By reviewing both recordings with the student, they can discuss

Meaningful Assessment: Focusing on the Whole Child

the progress made together. Not only does this provide clear evidence of growth, but it also helps inform next steps for both the teacher and student. More importantly, it offers a personalised perspective on a child's development rather than reducing them to a number in a cohort. Standardised test results alone cannot provide this depth of insight and often fail to capture the full picture of a child's progress.

Below is an example of what I believe an Ipsative recording method could look like. The example shows the individual progression of a year three child and although I have completely made up the information, it is based on areas of development that typically spring up in most classes.

Example: An Ipsative Approach Recording Table

Learner: Child A
Class/Year group: Year 3
Date of Birth: 3/06/2017
Term: Spring 1
Broad Focus Area: Literacy Skills

Table 11.1 A fabricated example of what an ipsative assessment recording table could look like

\multicolumn{7}{l}{**Key strengths:** Creative composition and innovative ideas. Shows good awareness of intended audience}
Date	Specific area of focus	Previous observation	Current observation	Consistency	Progress	Next step
---	---	---	---	---	---	---
01/3/25	Spelling: their/there/they're	Incorrect spelling and usage in writing	Used "their" correctly in a sentence today.	40%	Progress beginning to show	Create a their/there/they're game to play. Visual reminder
15/3/25	Reading fluency	Needing to rely on phonic sounds within each sentence	Read 50% of the words "on sight" without sounding.	50%	Significant progress made	Develop reading on and back technique – use close activities.

(Continued)

147

Table 11.1 (Continued)

Date	Specific area of focus	Previous observation	Current observation	Consistency	Progress	Next step
22/3/25	Reversal of "b" and "d"	Wrote "bab" instead of "dad"	Wrote dad correctly	100%	Achieved fully with use of a prompt aid.	Ensure learning is embedded without the need for a prompt.
5/4/25	Full stops	Wrote a whole page without one full stop	Wrote a set of instructions, including full stops and capital letters	60%	Significant progress made	Develop "Kung Fu" punctuation marks for other forms when reading work back.

Since discovering this approach, I firmly believe that ipsative assessment is a path worth exploring further. At the very least, I agree with Armstrong that teachers need to integrate it into their practice more frequently. While we regularly use formative, summative and standardised assessments, ipsative assessment remains largely underutilised. If we embraced it more widely, it could transform how students perceive their learning, fostering a sense of achievement, self-awareness and well-being. Imagine how rewarding it would be – not just for students, but for teachers as well – to witness and celebrate individual progress in such a meaningful way (Table 11.1).

References

Armstong, T. (2020, March 5). *What are ipsative assessments? 10 things to know.* [online] American Institute for Learning and Human Development Available at: https://www.institute4learning.com/2020/03/05/10-things-educators-should-know-about-ipsative-assessments/ [Accessed 5 June 2025].

BBC Sounds. (1979, October 27). *Welcome to Zscaler directory authentication.* [online] BBC.co.uk. Available at: https://www.bbc.co.uk/sounds/play/p009mwxx [Accessed 20 May 2025].

Dickens, J. (2020, February 26). DfE confirms September roll-out of baseline test. [online] *Schools Week*. Available at: https://schoolsweek.co.uk/dfe-claims-trial-shows-baseline-is-accurate-and-confirms-september-roll-out/ [Accessed 26 Nov. 2024].

Rosen, M. (2024, June 12). *This year's KS2 Grammar, punctuation and spelling test – analysed*. [online] Blogspot.com. Available at: https://michaelrosenblog.blogspot.com/2024/06/this-years-ks2-grammar-punctuation-and.html [Accessed 15 Jan. 2025].

Staufenberg, J. (2018, June 13). Schools in rich areas are more than twice as likely to be 'outstanding'. [online] *Schools Week*. Available at: https://schoolsweek.co.uk/schools-in-rich-areas-are-more-than-twice-as-likely-to-be-outstanding/ [Accessed 5 June 2025].

12 Conclusion

The way our current education system is does not allow for children to develop their true strengths nor pursue their greatest interests to the level at which it should. We need a society that is well-rounded and skilled in many different areas for it to function in a sustainable and effective way. With such a narrow focus concentrated on the core subjects of mathematics and literacy, we are essentially creating a society that is not varied enough and as a result there has been a depletion in certain types of industries such as our manufacturing industries in our country which are not what they once were. Could it be that the narrow educational focus has also had an effect on the mental health of children and young adults? Has our education system (especially the testing) led those who could have the potential to be extremely skilled in a more labour-intensive job to feel that they do not have much worth nor purpose in our society? Is there too much conscious and unconscious bias woven into the fabric of in our education system, failing to recognise and nurture talent in its rawest form?

We must move away from an education system that forces everyone into the same narrow mould, regardless of whether they fit or not. Too many children grow into adults believing they are failures with nothing to offer, simply because their unique talents and interests were overlooked. When we place the highest value only on reading, writing and mathematics, and constantly compare children to their peers, we risk crushing confidence and creativity. We overlook the value that other qualities and talents can bring, creating a sense of triviality to the subjects that are not a "main focus". For people who may be classed as "more hands on than academic" an illusion is created that they are "not good enough". Yet I firmly believe that every individual has something they are good at and something valuable to contribute.

Conclusion

The key is to help them discover it. We can do this simply by tuning into them, shifting the focus to what they can do rather than what they can't do yet and providing opportunities that spark their enthusiasm and state of "flow".

It concerns me that despite the abundance of research on diverse learning styles and multiple intelligences, this knowledge is not often referred to by the Department for Education when they bring in new initiatives for schools. Our current education system feels outdated and no longer fits with what is needed both in the short and long term for our society to thrive. Change and new initiatives have come and gone, education secretaries have dipped in and out and yet for lasting positive change to happen a consistent approach and a considerable amount of time are needed. Ultimately, we need educational reform that draws on the expertise of teachers, researchers and other educational professionals who have the experience, knowledge and understanding of how all children (neurotypical and neurodiverse) learn best. Reform should be a continuous process, where professionals share new findings and adapt their practices accordingly over time.

The curriculum feels as if it has become stagnant. Teaching is becoming narrower with ever more teaching to the test and unions reporting that disruptive behaviour, children's mental health issues and child absences are on the rise. We need to seriously question if our current systems are exacerbating the problems. What is evident is that they are clearly not helping. Education should be a joyous experience for all, but for many it does not appear to be that way. There is a max exodus from the system taking place in terms of teachers who are leaving the profession after many years (myself included) and pupils who are leaving the system to be homeschooled. All of this does not paint a picture of a system that is working effectively. In truth it is a system that is on its knees.

While some form of assessment is necessary to inform next steps and to encourage progression, our current regimented assessment approach is, quite frankly, damaging in the primary sector. Children are subjected to a constant cycle of testing, levelling and comparison from an early age, which places undue pressure on both learners and teachers. This high-stakes environment often prioritises performance over genuine understanding and discourages risk-taking, creativity and a love of learning. Instead of nurturing curiosity and personal growth, we are pushing children to meet uniform benchmarks that don't reflect the diverse ways in which they develop and thrive. Assessment should be a tool for support, not a mechanism of stress or judgement. As this book has explored, there are alternative, less pressured ways to assess children, approaches that offer richer, more meaningful insights into who they are as learners, rather than reducing them to a number or another statistic. Every child should feel they can achieve. Every child should have the opportunity to explore their passions. Every child should be included and valued. No child should be reduced to a meaningless set of numbers.

We are all unique individuals who learn, express ourselves and think in different ways. Yet the current education system, in many ways, pushes us towards a uniform way of thinking. From a young age, children are often discouraged from thinking differently if their perspective doesn't align with the mainstream. But it is precisely those who think outside the box who have driven some of the most extraordinary advances in human knowledge and understanding. Without them, we might still believe the Earth is flat, or lack any conceptual understanding of evolution, or be without the medical breakthroughs that have transformed lives – all because someone dared to challenge accepted ideas.

Extraordinary things happen when we allow ourselves to question, to wonder, and to step beyond the boundaries of conventional thought. Sadly, this natural curiosity seems to diminish as we grow older. Anyone who has spent time with a young child knows the endless stream of "why" questions – a beautiful, instinctive pursuit of understanding that we should strive to preserve, not suppress. Questioning is not just a developmental phase; it's a crucial life skill. Critical thinking forms the foundation of informed decision-making, personal growth and meaningful societal progress. Without it, we risk accepting flawed ideas, repeating past mistakes and overlooking opportunities for positive change. That's why it is so essential to value and support those in our society who challenge preconceived ideas. They are the innovators and trailblazers without whom progress would grind to a halt.

Governments need to put greater trust in educational professionals and be guided by those with genuine experience, expertise and a solid grounding in educational research before implementing changes or introducing new legislation. Too often, major decisions about education are made by those far removed from the realities of the classroom. A notable example is Michael Gove's tenure as Education Secretary, during which sweeping reforms were introduced with insufficient meaningful consultation with teachers or educational experts. His focus on a knowledge-rich, exam-driven curriculum and the absence of frameworks that support creativity and professional autonomy have had lasting impacts many of which are still being felt in primary education today. This top-down approach has led to missed opportunities to create a more balanced, inclusive and child-centred system. Lasting improvement will only come when policy is shaped in genuine partnership with those who understand children best: the educators who work with them every day. While Government recognises that there is a problem with teacher retention, their answer seems to be to entice and fast track new recruits into teaching. Considering that teaching is a skill that is honed over time, it is a tragedy that they are not delving into and uncovering the reasons behind a teacher shortage and trying to fix it and retain teachers. It is rather like trying to fill up a bucket with a hole in it. When an experienced teacher leaves, all of the knowledge and skills gained through years of practice evaporates – it will not be passed down to early career teachers (ECTs). As a result, we are left with a less robust and unsustainable system. Yes, we need more teachers, but more needs to be done to retain the experienced ones. The teachers need to feel listened to and above all valued, not just by senior leaders within their school but by the Government, the wider public and portrayed in a better light in the media.

On a positive note, there are changes that we can make, based on the research out there about how learners learn best. Innovative educational approaches such as project-based learning, experiential learning and personalised learning plans can cater to individual strengths and interests. For example, Finland's education system, renowned for its flexibility and focus on providing a well-rounded offering to students, already embraces many similar methods that have been explored in this book and as a result has seen positive outcomes in student engagement and performance. Incorporating more vocational training and practical skills into the curriculum can also address the gap that has been created in modern times. Countries like Germany and Switzerland have successful apprenticeship programmes that integrate classroom learning with hands-on experience, providing students with a clear path to various careers.

The benefits of outdoor learning are well-documented, and this book explores them in some depth. While younger children often enjoy regular access to rich, well-equipped outdoor environments, opportunities for older pupils to learn outside are far more limited. This needs to change! The days of children being confined to their desks for most of their school lives must become a thing of the past. We need to get them moving, exploring and engaging with the world around them, sparking their curiosity and reigniting a deep, energetic desire to learn. At a time when we are becoming increasingly disconnected from the natural world, it is more important than ever to rebuild that relationship. We need the generations to come to bring new ways of thinking, in terms of sustainable living. To restore our planet, we need knowledge, yes, but more than that, we need to care. And it is through meaningful experiences and genuine connection that care is born. Passion leads to purpose, and purpose leads to action.

The ideas shared in this book are by no means a definitive solution to the complex challenges facing education today. However, I hope they offer a spark of inspiration and provoke thought about the new directions we might take. We often hear that the system is broken, yet rarely do we hear concrete, constructive suggestions for how to fix it. What is clear is that we are in urgent need of a paradigm shift – one that is guided not by political agendas, but by robust research and the insights of those who know education best: the teachers working on the front lines every day.

It is my hope that radical changes will be made in the not-so-distant future, taking into account the extensive research available. All children should feel that they can and will excel in something during their primary school journey, creating a lifelong love of learning that continues into their adult lives, a sense of purpose and improved mental health.

Ultimately, an education system that recognises and nurtures each child's unique genius will lead to a more diverse, skilled and mentally healthy society.

Index

Note: **Bold** page numbers refer to tables and *italic* page numbers refer to figures.

Academies Act 8
academy 7; autonomy 8; *vs.* council-maintained schools 8; *vs.* local authority-maintained schools 8; policy shift 8
adult literacy 36
The Alps Approach (Smith and Call) 31
Armstrong, N. 90
Armstrong, T. 146–148
art education 13–15
artistic play 12; *see also* play
assessment: and documentation 111–112; end-of-term 145; international 60; ipsative 146–148, **147–148**; meaningful 138–148; standardised 53
attention and physical play 73–77
attention-seeking behaviour 45; *see also* behaviour
Augmentative and Alternative Communication (ACC) 33
autism masking 27

balanced approach: progressive methods 37; to reading instruction 40
behaviour 3; anti-social 60; attention-seeking 45; challenging 41–49; as communication 44, 45; controlling pupil 45–46; disruptive 46–48, 57, 151; issues outdoor learning 79; masking 27; outdated methods 33; personal emotion 46; positive reinforcement 57–58; restorative approach 41–42, 46
Bell, A. G. 87
The BFG (Dahl) 115
Biff, Chip and Kipper books 58, 143
brain development 15–18, *16*
Branson, R. 6
British Sign Language (BSL) 34
Brown, P. 106; *The Wild Robot* 106–107
Buckinghamshire Government 5

Call, N. 31; *The Alps Approach* 31
CBeebies 139
Centre for Neurological Science 127
child-led learning 37–40, 133; challenges in large classes 51–53; creativity and 18; essential skills 38; Forest School 25; monitoring 52; statistical data 53–54; structure and expectations 49; and teacher-led learning 13; *see also* learning
chunking method 57–58
Churchill, W. 141

Index

cognitive behavioural therapy (CBT) 134
Collins, S. 104; *When Charlie McButton Lost Power* 104–105
Columbus, C. 90
communication: behaviour management 45, 46, 56; for hearing individuals 34; verbal 34
continuous provision 114–122; challenges 118–121; drawback 118; effective approach 119; flow 121–122; implementation 116–117; independence 117; innovative methods 119; planning for 118; real-time feedback 120; structured timetabled approach 114
corporal punishment 3, 41
counterproductive approach 29–30
COVID-19 1
Cowell, S. 6
creativity 12; activity 70–71; art education 13–15; imagination and 124; and innovation 96; with intrinsic motivation 25; and play 13; and practical arts 4
critical thinking 152
Csikszentmihalyi, M. 20
curriculum: adaptable learning paths 111; aims-led 83; anecdotal records 112; assessment and documentation 111–112; balance of routine and freedom 110–111; broad and balanced 9, 83, 85, **92–95**; collaboration and group work 111; creating and implementing 111–112; creating content 84; dynamic and creative 84; flexibility and adaptability 111; key maths skills 110; learning environments and 26; learning portfolios 111–112; phonics and reading skills 109; professional development and support 112–113; reflective practices 112; restrictive 2, 132; spelling focus input 110; statutory and routine 109–111; teacher observations 112; *see also* behaviour; national curriculum; thematic learning

Dahl, R. 115, 141; *The BFG* 115
data: and measuring performance 53–54; numerical 138, 140, 142–147; statistical 53–54
deeper learning 50, 57; *see also* learning
Deng, G. 80; *Journal of International Medical Research* 80
Desert Island Discs 141
Dickens, J. 144
A Different Way to Learn (Fisher) 28, 132–133
disruptive behaviour 46–48, 57, 151; *see also* behaviour
diverse learning styles 151
Dogger (Hughes) 89
Donaldson, J. 98; *The Gruffalo* 98–99
Donelan, M. 9
Doyle, C. 107; *Sherlock Holmes* 107–108
Duddle, J. 100; *The Pirates Next Door* 100

Eat your Greens, Goldilocks (Smallman) 89
Eaves, E. 100; *How to catch a dragon* 100–101
Education Secretary 9–10
education system 1, 150–151; aims of 84; challenges 30; elementary 3; Finland's education system 153; and gender roles 3–4; national curriculum and statutory tests 117; revolutionised literacy 39; spoon-feeds knowledge and skills 133; statistical data 53–54; *see also* specific education
Eichler, W. 8
"The 1870 Education Act" 2

Index

Einstein, A. 141
elementary school 3; *see also* schools
Emotionally Based School Avoidance 26
Ephgrave, A. 132
Even, D. T. 123
extrinsic motivation 51; *see also* motivation

"fight" or "flight" response 15, 31
Finland's education system 153; *see also* education system
Finnegan's Wake (Joyce) 115
The Firework Maker's Daughter (Pullman) 124, 125, *126*
Fisher, N. 28–29, 132–133; *A Different Way to Learn* 132–133
flow 3, 20–25; absorption in activities 21; in action 24; and brains function 23; in classroom 20; continuous provision 121–122; in everyday activities 22–23; Forest School and 24–25; in homework 57, 61; in occupations and hobbies 21; outdoor environments 80–81; planning for 123–137; principles 116; project-based learning approach 125; sports performance 21; teaching and lesson planning 21
Forest School: child-led learning 25; flow 24–25; growth mindset 24; impact of outdoor learning 64–79, 81, 118
Free School Meals (FSM) 5
free schools 8–9; *see also* schools

gender equality 3–5
George's Marvellous Medicine 66
Gillard, D. 2
Goldsworthy, A. 25
Goleman, D. 20, 23; *Working with Emotional Intelligence* 20, 23
Gove, M. 8, 115, 152
Graham, B. 99; *Max* 99–100

grammar schools 5, 6; *see also* schools
growth mindset 24
The Gruffalo (Donaldson) 98–99

hands-on activities: and screen-based experiences 17–18
Hansen, D. 38
Harry Potter and the Philosopher's Stone (Rowling) 108–109
Hart, C. 100; *How to catch a dragon* 100–101
health benefit: outdoor learning 79–80
Higham, R. 9
high-functioning autism: apple carving activity 67; cooperative creative play 67–68; creativity 65; distraction technique 66; social and emotional skills 65–69; storytelling 66
home economics 4
homework 55; challenges 55; child autonomy 58; child-initiated activity and set 58; for engagement 55–61; extracurricular activities programme 59–60; flow in 57, 61; parental role in 56; project-based 55; quality and quantity 58; reading skills 58–59; screen-based tasks 56; trends 60–61; UK vs. Finland 60
How to catch a dragon (Hart and Eaves) 100–101
Hughes, S. 89; *Dogger* 89
Hughes, T.: *The Iron Man* 101–102

imaginative play 71; *see also* play
inclusivity: curriculum 4; evolution 40–41
individual child and progress, outdoor learning 64–77; attention and physical play 73–77; high-functioning autism, social and emotional skills 65–69; resilience and risk-taking 69–73
information gathering approach 145–146
Ingram, J. 53

Index

innovative educational approaches 153
intellectual development 12, 15, 18
interdisciplinary learning 91–96;
92–95; community and society 91, 92, 95–96; conflict and resolution 91; ethics and philosophy 91; futures and possibilities 91; power of media 91; scientific revolutions 91; *see also* learning
interdisciplinary teams 34
intrinsic motivation 25, 28, 39, 51, 61, 116, 133; *see also* motivation
investigative learning model 96–109
investigatory approach 86, 112, 113
ipsative assessment 146–148, **147–148**; *see also* assessment
The Iron Man (Hughes) 101–102

Journal of International Medical Research (Zhang and Deng) 80
Joyce, J. 115; *Finnegan's Wake* 115

Keegan, G. 8
Kendall, E. 27

Lambert, D. 78; *The National Curriculum Outdoors* 78
learning: behaviours 29; counterproductive and spontaneous 29; curiosity and 29–30; deeper 50, 57; developmental readiness for 31; individualised and adaptive 85; interactive white-boards 56; outdoor *see* outdoor learning; passive 141; purposeful 47; self-directed 116; tablet-based 56; through play 12–15; trauma impact on 31–32
Lennon, J. 141
literacy: adult 36; phonics instruction 39–40; revolutionised literacy education 39; thematic learning 88–90
Literacy and Numeracy hour 3
local authorities 7–8

London Mathematical Society 127
Luton, F. 117

Maclean, P. 15, *16*
Makaton 33–34
masking behaviours 27; *see also* behaviour
maths: anxiety 127; teaching 126–129
Max (Graham) 99–100
McHugh, K. 114
mental health 27, 62, 134–135, 142, 150, 151
mindfulness activities 89
Minecraft game 4
misbehaviour 45; *see also* behaviour
Morin, A. 17
motivation 24, 143; extrinsic 51; intrinsic 25, 28, 39, 51, 61, 116, 133
multi-academy trusts (MATs) 7–8
Murphy, J.: *The Worst Witch* 102
myopia 79–80

Naiman, L. 13
national curriculum 6–8; challenges 85; flexibility 85; interdisciplinary learning 91–96; investigatory tasks 86; purpose 83; safeguards 85; and statutory tests 117; thematic learning *see* thematic learning; uniformity of 84; White's perspective 83–84; *see also* curriculum
The National Curriculum Outdoors (Lambert, Roberts and Waite) 78
national literacy trust 36, 58–59
The Nature Fix (Williams) 62
neurodiverse learners/neurodiversity 27, 133; challenges 35; developmental differences 31; prioritise needs 35; school expectations and challenges 28–29; sensory hypersensitivity in 28; Special Educational Needs (SEN) and 32
neuroscience 15, 116
neurotypical learners 29, 31, 133

Index

Nightingale, F. 90
non-linear learning 13; *see also* learning
numerical data 138, 140, 142–147

obedience: intrinsic motivation 28, 51
OFSTED 2, 7, 119
one-size-fits-all approach 31–33
online learning 56; *see also* learning
Osborne, M. P. 104; *Vacation under the volcano* 104
outdoor learning: attention and physical play 73–77; behaviour issues 79; benefits 62–81; boosting health and well-being 79–80; creative arts 63; flow 80–81; Forest School impact 64–79, 81, 118; high-functioning autism, social and emotional skills 65–69; individual child and progress 64–77; inner city schools 78; Lambert's 78; physical activity 118–119; into primary curriculum 78; resilience and risk-taking 69–73; spending time in 62, 80; well-being and 63–64; *see also* learning

Parks, R. 40, 90
passive learning 141; *see also* learning
Peal, R. 37, 38, 42, 43; *Progressively Worse: The Burden of Bad Ideas in British Schools* 37, 42
permissive philosophy 42
Peter Pan story 97–98
phonics 39–40
physical activity: outdoor learning 118–119
pigeonholing 140–142
The Pirates Next Door (Duddle) 100
PISA cycles 53
"planning in the moment" approach 131–135
play: attention and 73–77; brain development 58; creativity and 13; hands-on activities 17; imaginative 71; importance of 12–15; learning through 12–15, 55; peg puzzle 17; time engaging in 116
policy reform 35
positive reinforcement 48, 58
primary school: continuous provision 122; in England 37; experience working in 114–115; outdoor learning 80; project-based homework 55–56; working hours 1; *see also* schools
problem-solving skill 12–18; play and 12–15
progressive investigative learning model 96–109; further challenge 103–109
Progressively Worse: The Burden of Bad Ideas in British Schools (Peal) 37, 42
progressive methods 6, 37, 42; balanced approach 37–38; evolving evidence and practice 38; Peal's critique 38
project-based homework 55; *see also* homework
project-based learning approach 125
PSHCE (Personal, Social, Health and Citizenship Education) 49, 96
Pullman, P. 124; *The Firework Maker's Daughter* 124, 125, *126*
Pupil Premium Funding 5
purposeful learning 47; *see also* learning

reading skills, at home 58–59
Ready Kids Occupational Therapy 47
Realistic Mathematics Education (RME) 129
Reception Baseline Assessment (RBA) 144–145
reflective practices 112
reluctant learners 57
resilience: collaborative creativity and confidence 71–72; confidence and participation 69; creativity activity 70–71; and risk-taking 69–73; teamwork, creativity and storytelling 72

Index

restorative approach 41–42, 46
restrictive curriculum 2, 132; see also curriculum
revolutionised literacy education 39
Roberts, M. 78; *The National Curriculum Outdoors* 78
Roblox game 4
role play 128; see also play
Rosen, M. 88, 115, 142; *We're Going on a bear Hunt* 88
rote learning 2, 18
Rowling, J. K. 108; *Harry Potter and the Philosopher's Stone* 108–109

SATs and league tables 7
school improvement 7; effectiveness 9; evidence-based strategies 9
schools: artificial consequences and uniform rules in 28; comprehensive 5; grammar 5, 6; grammar vs. comprehensive/secondary 5; restorative practices 41–42; restrictive curriculum 2, 132
screen-based experiences: hands-on activities and 17–18
secondary schools 5; working hours 1
Secondary Transfer Test 5
self-directed learning 116; see also learning
sensory hypersensitivity: in neurodiverse children 28
Severs, A. 116
Shake It Off (Swift) 110
Shakibaie, S. 47
Sherlock Holmes (Doyle) 107–108
Smallman, S. 89; *Eat your Greens, Goldilocks* 89
Smith, A. 31; *The Alps Approach* 31
Smith, D. K.: *The Waterhorse* 105–106
special educational needs and disabilities (SEND) 1, 26–35, 50; assistive technologies 35; and neurodiversity 32; policy reform and 35

spider diagram method 123
Spielman, A. 2
spontaneous learning 29; see also learning
statistical data: education system 53–54
Staufenberg, J. 142
STEM (Science, Technology, Engineering and Mathematics) education 4
stimming 27
Sugar, A. 6
Summerhill's GCSE results 38
Sunflower picture (Gogh) 13–15
Swift, T. 110; *Shake It Off* 110
Szucs, D. 127

Tapestry 144–146
teacher-centred approach 6
teacher-led learning 13; see also child-led learning
teacher professional judgement 7
teacher workload and well-being 1
TeachMate AI 86, 112
technology: assistive 35; overreliance on 18
Thatcher, M. 6, 83
thematic learning 86; art 87; framework 86; geography 87; interdisciplinary approach 86, 91–96; investigatory tasks 86; language arts 87; literacy 88–90; mathematics 87; numeracy 88–90; science 87; weather and natural habitats 88
themes as central pillars 86, 88–91; numeracy and literacy 88–90
The Three Little Pigs story 97
Trainspotting (Welsh) 115
trial-and-error methods 17, 18
Tripartite System 5
Triune Brain Model 15–18, *16*
Tweddle, B. 138

Vacation under the volcano (Osborne) 104
Van Gogh, V. 13–15

160

Index

verbal communication 34; *see also* communication
visual, auditory and kinesthetic (VAK) learning styles 32

Waite, S. 78; *The National Curriculum Outdoors* 78
The Waterhorse (Smith) 105–106
well-being: nature and 63–64; outdoor learning 79–80; physical and emotional 63; teacher workload and 1
Welsh, I. 115; *Trainspotting* 115
We're Going on a bear Hunt (Rosen) 88
When Charlie McButton Lost Power (Collins) 104–105
White, J. 83–84
The Wild Robot (Brown) 106–107
Williams, F. 62; *The Nature Fix* 62
Wilson, R. 84
Wiltshire, S. 138
Working with Emotional Intelligence (Goleman) 20, 23
The Worst Witch (Murphy) 102

Zhang, J. 80; *Journal of International Medical Research* 80

For Product Safety Concerns and Information please contact our EU
representative GPSR@taylorandfrancis.com
Taylor & Francis Verlag GmbH, Kaufingerstraße 24, 80331 München, Germany

www.ingramcontent.com/pod-product-compliance
Lightning Source LLC
Chambersburg PA
CBHW071821230426
43670CB00013B/2526